FOREWORD

AUTHOR'S PURPOSE

I write this book to account for all that I have witnessed in the inner-city of Baltimore; a place where black minorities have the hardest plight than any other ethnic counterpart. Plenty of the struggle is attributed to the socio-economic divide on the basis of social class and race. Part of the struggle is self-induced and/or self-inflicted. A lot of the struggle is inevitably perpetuated, nearly inescapable, and hard to be avoided, as it circulates through the inner-city like a demonizing wicked wind. Many blacks cannot help but to become entangled in the rapture of the struggle. The word, struggle, itself takes on a ubiquitous meaning which has no format. However, Baltimore's inner-city struggle, includes a range of socioeconomic issues (e.g. poverty, drug addiction, disease, broken families, black-on-black violence, mass incarceration, inferior education, gunplay, teenage pregnancy, downtrodden communities, limited resources/outreach; etc.).

In a typical sense, one may say that this type of condition exists everywhere in every major inner-city where blacks are prevalent. I do not contest the truth of this matter. However, I am specifying the social conditions of those in my own backyard. It is so easy to generalize the struggle of black urban communities;

but significance, authenticity, and individualism is compromised when this is done. Therefore, I choose to signify the people of one particular city. A people of their own cultural customs, values, colloquialisms, social qualms, and hardships. I do not wish to emulsify and overlap the struggles of the black inner-city of Baltimore with the other black inner-cities elsewhere. I understand when it comes to the inner-city, most of the blacks` struggles are thematic and synonymous as those that have been outlined in the above paragraph. The ingredients may be similar but the recipe is not always the same. For instance, the way that Baltimore has come to be in today's present time does not account for how other black inner-cities may have wound up in the same predicament. Regardless of the similarities or not, a social condition suffered by a particular race of people in a particular place in the world, deserves to be brought to center by anyone who is willing, and bold enough to paint the picture.

Therefore, it is my pleasure to present to you a very detailed and accurate depiction of what is occurring in the inner-city of Baltimore as it pertains to the black minority. My intentions are to shine light on these situations, by exploring every social avenue that leads to our own destruction, and downfall as black leaders to the youth. The black youth are those who will suffer in these torn communities of Baltimore. Role models in the hood are far and few in between. When the youth depend on nurturing from the streets, they become potentially at risk to become another statistic and product of their environment. They're exposed to so many different social ailments in the inner-city of Baltimore. Even the foods offered in the community are a form of biological and chemical warfare. The schools they attend, lack the resources acquired to produce proficient scholars and future leaders.

I will address these issues of inner-city drug use (addiction and distribution) amongst blacks, because this particular issue sets the format of experience and outcome for so many black youths. Drug use in the inner-city is generational and perpetual. Therefore, the effects of generational drug use in the inner-city black communities will be explored.

A community cannot save itself from its social deficiencies without the backing and help of its local and state governing officials. Baltimore officials' negligence within the black community will not go unchecked, and will be addressed within this book as best as research supports and provides. Solutions, along with implications for socioeconomic restoration will be outlined in order to motivate the masses of leaders and influencers to galvanize resourceful strategies and tactics for change.

This book is a precursor and introduction into researching and exploring sociological issues as it pertains to blacks or African American's. *A Rage in Baltimore*, has challenged me to vow to continue on research regarding black matters in order to shine light upon the state of blacks in America nationwide.

CHAPTER 1

NUTRITIONAL WARFARE IN THE URBAN COMMUNITY

Six years residing in Baltimore's inner-city community, I have witnessed an abundance of corner stores from block-to-block. It is beneficial stores of convenience exist in the Baltimore inner-city. It saves time and energy, spent traveling to a market outside of the black community. Another positive attribute is that many of the corner stores are black owned. It is great to see our community members sprouting businesses within our communities.

However, the food that most corner stores offer in the black community are extremely unhealthy, processed, overly saturated with artificial flavoring, loaded with sodium and sugar, and contributory to most of the diseases that blacks are at risk for developing: These diseases associated with poor diet include; diabetes, high blood pressure/ hypertension, high HDL (bad cholesterol), and atherosclerosis.

In addition to corner stores, many inner-city parents within the black community leave their children to chance their health and diet by allowing the abundance of take-out or carryout food in the household. The chicken box is a real popular dish served at Baltimore city carry-outs. The chicken box consists of a portion of wings with a choice of fries and/or roll, as a side. I see many children flooding these carry-outs to order a chicken box during dinner hours. It is not crucial to eat this type of food once or twice a week; however, the abundance and consistency of consumption paves the way toward obesity.

According to the State of Obesity (2015), 20.2% of black youth are obese in the United States. The State of Obesity organization also indicates that "82% of black women are overweight or obese compared to 63.2% of white women" (2015). As a whole, 47.8% of black adults in the U.S. are overweight as compared to 32.6% of white adults in the U.S. that are overweight (State of Obesity, 2015). These results indicate that our black community as a whole are struggling with healthy dieting. Black inner-city youths are suffering because of the lack of healthy food choices in their environment and household. It's obvious that most black inner-city households are filled with foods of convenience. This means our children are eating indoors the same way they would if they purchased junk food from the corner store.

There is a strong need for nutritional education in black communities within Baltimore City. The scarcity of high quality supermarkets presents a nutritional disadvantage, because stores of convenience offer inadequate choices of healthy foods, if any. Years of perpetuated non-practice of exercise, unhealthy dieting, and lack of health consciousness promotes the tradition of passing these inferior eating and dieting habits down to our black youth. Being tagged as overweight or obese is the result of what we eat, more so, than the portions we consume. Regardless of BMI measurements, the main importance is what we are eating, and what we are feeding to our children.

What we consume in terms of nourishment is representative of our culinary ideology. Culinary ideology is your household food culture: (a) the types of foods you eat, (b) the way you prepare your food and (c) the nutritional quality of your food. Many black inner-city households culinary ideology is influenced by the types of food that is available within their environment. It is no mistake that black inner-city community's culinary ideology is convoluted and polluted by Americanized cuisine.

Analyzing American Food Culture

Americanized cuisine is a bastardize hybridization and conglomerate mixture of some Western and Eastern European cuisine. American food is primarily derivative of the traditional cuisines of Eastern European immigrants that migrated from their countries during 19th and early 20th centuries: the time of global war and social injustice. They were the first to experience the effects of government project housing in America. Just as many minorities and blacks today in project housing, many Eastern Europeans were placed in huge buildings cluttered with one apartment atop of another piled to the sky. This ethnic group was social-economically stratified and marginalized like many blacks and other minorities. They were once the sufferers and victims of impoverished housing communities within the major inner-cities of America. The term ghetto is associated and coined after those first and second generation immigrants that migrated from their failing European countries into the hoods or America. Ghettoization was used to describe the social-economic imbalance and deplorable mistreatment and the condition of Eastern Europeans in America. Most of them could not afford traditional foods of a greater quality. Therefore, they worked with what they were able to render to feed their families. Although incomparable in terms of social disparity, their struggle is somewhat relative to the black enslaved and freed ancestors, that had to make whatever they could, out of the scraps handed down from their white oppressor's plate.

Contrary to the convenience cuisine epidemic, initiatives are being made in Baltimore's inner-city. Numerous individuals from all walks of life have volunteered to cultivate "urban gardens" in various cities within Baltimore. The goal is to develop and distribute healthy foods throughout the urban communities. This development of urban gardens makes good quality foods accessible to the inner-city communities. Furthermore, individuals within the community become knowledgeable about agriculture and crop production. There is also an economic advantage because money stays within the community.

Denise Morris

There are corner stores in the inner-city that do promote and encourage healthy eating. I have seen quite a few that have fresh fruits and vegetables on display. It would be awesome if their counterparts would follow the lead. However, the individuals within the community must request these items. The corner stores are businesses; supply-and-demand is how they purchase orders and make money. If the community fails to express the desire for better food, there is no need to expect inner-city vendors to create an inventory for quality foods.

Case studies conducted specifically in Baltimore's inner-city communities have proven black youths are substituting nutritional meals with junk foods. Dennisuk et al., (2015) conducted a study on 242 black youths from ages 10-14 years. The youth were selected from low-income communities in Baltimore. The purpose of the study was to determine the food purchasing habits of inner-city black youth. Dennisuk et al., (2015) concluded:

Youth reported spending an average of $3.96 on foods and beverages in a typical day. Corner stores were the most frequently visited food source (youth made purchases at these stores an average of 2.0 times per week). Chips, candy, and soda were the most commonly purchased items, with youth purchasing these an average of 2.5, 1.8, and 1.4 times per week, respectively. Older age was associated with more money spent on food in a typical day ($p<0.01$). (p. 625)

Developing Healthier Solutions

Separating or reducing the junk foods from the household can improve the quality of dieting in black inner-city households. Foods of convenience should not be a dominant source of nutrition. We live in a world where we can utilize the Internet to find out anything we want. There are apps that link us to our favorite activities. There are also apps that inform us of healthy eating practices and various exercises to improve our lifestyle. Inner-city programs that are free are also offered throughout the city. There are usually non-profit and/or grassroots organizations that offer information regarding food and nutrition. Some even offer the community courses on nutrition, free of charge.

The black inner-city community must be aware of the associated health risks that impact blacks. The black inner-city household can achieve significant improvements in health by replacing traditionally poor eating habits with health conducive eating habits. The transformation of food culture can lead to more inventive ways of food preparation. For instance, how we eat is important to consider besides what we eat. Excessive and unwanted calories can be avoided by choosing to bake meals instead of frying. Steaming foods is better than microwaving foods, because steaming preserves the nutrients within foods.

Seeking professional guidance is useful as well. Consult with your doctor or nutritionist about ways to maintain a fit and healthy lifestyle. Most likely your doctor has a long list of your health issues or areas you need improvement in health wise. Too often, we wait to be diagnosed with diabetes, high blood pressure or hypertension. The elders who raised our parents did not readily go to the doctors for things of this nature. Some of our own parents have followed this type of behavior. In this day and age, there is more information and services equally available unto the black community. Many of our elders (grandparents) were disenfranchised or turned away because of the racial climate of the era in which they lived.

Implications for Researchers, Concerning Black Inner-City Dieting

Empirical research gathered on Baltimore's inner-city black youth's eating habits indicate several different factors. Spending habits are synonymous with affordability or income. Secondly, household income is synonymous with the types of foods that are present within Baltimore's black inner-city households. For instance, most of the households within these communities are low-income. This means parents may only have the option of purchasing inexpensive foods that are usually processed, and are an unhealthy source of nutrition. Subsequently, low-income is detrimental and attributive to the purchasing habits in black inner-city communities. Single parented households are potentially another factor, since an additional source of income can aid in affording healthier foods.

Furthermore, super marketing distribution practices in black inner-city communities within Baltimore consist of a target market that buy from manufactures that produce low quality food products. It is very rare to find an abundance of organic food products in these communities. Common brand supermarkets (e.g. Shopper's, Safeway, and Giant Foods) available but limited in most Baltimore black inner-city communities overcharge for organic food products that are available in their stores. Overall, these particular lower income households are burdened with the plague of poor dieting food choices, due to the lack of available inner-city markets that provide healthier foods at affordable prices. Researchers must develop more case studies based around food inequality in black inner-city communities; these types of communities are being disenfranchised upon the bases of their social-economic status.

The Food and Drug Administration (FDA) needs to consider the value of closely inspecting and monitoring grocery stores and markets in the urban community. It is no surprise that bad produce is often shipped to black communities and purchased by food merchants for a cheap price. In addition, the consumer in the urban community that purchases poor quality foods, may fail to see the dangers in purchasing the lesser brand, because it is given at a discounted or buy one get one free sale. In this case, expense trumps quality. The food is affordable at the cost of one's health. I have witnessed two non-black owned mom-and-pop grocery stores close in Baltimore city in 2016. These stores had major violations that were FDA unacceptable. To no one's surprise, these same stores have been open for decades. Many black members of the community, including myself, have been in these places and seen the spoiled meat. The smell upon entering these places would make you sick to your stomach. However, the FDA have let these food merchants serve poison to the poor urban black communities for years. The FDA headquarters is located approximately 45 minutes away in Silver Spring, MD. There is no reason why they should be elusive in communities so closely neighbored.

CHAPTER 2

DRUG USE AND BALTIMORE'S BLACK YOUTH

Baltimore was once declared the heroin capital of the United States. Crack cocaine has also had its run in the city of Baltimore. In most black inner-city communities, drugs are more prevalent and available than quality education, employment opportunities, recreational or youth centers, and sufficient housing. Like many inner cities, Baltimore is still suffering from the lingering effects from the government's successful attempt to push drugs into the black community.

Shaming to believe, our very own government conspired on a nationwide level, to destroy the black community. It is also shaming to know, they imposed harsh drug laws against those in the inner-city that distributed the same drugs that they could have never accessed on their own. However, the government smuggled tons of drugs from other countries; making it readily accessible to the black community. During the Raegan and Bush era, the war on drugs was initiated, and blacks suffered the harshest jail time and penalties. It is amazing how the government created an epidemic of drug ridden inner cities across the nation; creating a system that both poisoned and punished its victims. The evidence thereof, can still be seen in this present day and time.

13

Denise Morris

Heroin still remains a huge problem in Baltimore city. Its users are getting younger and younger. There are many young adults and adolescents who use heroin. Typically, a minor's first drug experience would be marijuana. Nowadays, kids are bypassing weed on the verge to an even higher high. Many black adolescents in Baltimore's inner-city have family histories of generational drug use. In many cases, these adolescents may even live in the household with a parent or relative who abuses drugs or narcotics. Inner-city households infested with drug abusers are no place for a child. In fact, the child is more susceptible and capable of potentially using drugs, because of the presence of drugs or drug addicts in the household. Furthermore, the drug addicted relative serves as both an example, and a victim of the dope game that our former government bodies introduced.

Baltimore's black inner-city youth run the risk of becoming the new face of heroin. They run the risk of becoming that drug addicted parent or relative in the household. The reality of these black adolescents fate should alarm every parent in America, regardless of race or class. No one wants to fathom the thought of their child becoming an addict and washed up adult. A trap has been set long ago. At first, their parents or elder relatives were the future. Those who fell into the dope trap are either addicts or recovering addicts in this present day and time. Their parents or relatives may have also been products of the dope trap.

A home with drug users and drug abusers is a broken home. This why there are so many black adolescents in the foster care system in Baltimore. The foster care system has become the new slave auction for our youth. There is money to be made juggling a child from house to house. A lot of youth in the foster care system suffer from cognitive, developmental, and emotional disorders. One reason, may stem from being with total strangers instead of parents or relatives. Secondly, there are some cruel foster parents who shouldn't even be able to obtain licensing to raise children. Child and Family Services (CFS), overlooks these things, like countless other governmental child and protective services nationwide. A lot of foster care children in the inner-city are diagnosed with having disorders, and then medically treated. If this is not a gateway to drug use, what is? So, the government will find a way to introduce drugs back into the black community. Whether legally or illegally. The system will also find a way to get our inner-city children doped one way or another.

Drugs are the reason and blame for many existing social and economic disparities in Baltimore City. There does exist several drug recovery programs in Baltimore that are profitable and beneficial to addicts seeking recovery. However, after years and decades of use, so much is missed. Many have missed out on raising and rearing their offspring. Consequently, many of their children fall to drugs, because of the pain of neglect. Their children may not fall victim to drugs; instead, they have a chip on their shoulder or grudge, because drugs have taken their parents away from them.

I have heard many individuals who are ignorant to the effects of drugs say that the drug addicted individual chose that lifestyle, and it's all their fault. It may have been a choice, but one must also be cognizant of the options and circumstances available within that person's environment. The term "product of my own environment" should be taken into account when analyzing the nature of those who chose drugs. Poverty is indicative of crime, and crime is indicative of drugs, and various other related ills that stem from poverty. There are certain social ingredients within impoverished communities that are designed to make its dwellers fail and self-destruct. Drug abusers, often turn to drugs because of this despair. Many cannot afford prevention intervention therapy, and/or they are not even educated on the benefits of therapy. In the black community, therapy is often perceived as a weakness or "white thing". Drugs are a way for many to self-medicate. Unlike therapy, drugs are very accessible in impoverished communities. Baltimore's inner-city is littered with small time drug dealers, who are also a products of their environment. Most of the drug dealers deal drugs within the same community in which they reside. They also get high as well. They are also self-medicating. Drugs are a form of "ghetto therapy". Many addicts aren't getting high for thrill. They're getting high to escape the pain and worthlessness that they feel. In an actual mental health profession, a therapist would render a diagnoses, then the psychiatrist, according to the diagnoses, may render a medication or prescription to assist with lessening the symptoms of the disorder. On the street corner, the dealer is the psychiatrist. The addict or customer is the patient. The drug is the medication and therapy.

Medication for those Addicted to Heroin

The origins of Buprenorphine as its introduction goes is that it was the first opioid depressant drug approved through the Drug Addiction Treatment Act of 2000 (DATA, 2000; Genberg et al., 2013). Since, its inception, Buprenorphine, has been panhandled or exchanged on the streets amongst addicts and/or heroin users, either to self-medicate or exchange for more heroin. Methadone (another form of prescription drug for heroin users), is mishandled the same way.

The evidence of the mishandling of opiate drugs intended to help heroin addicts, reveals the inconsistency between drug treatment clinics as it pertains to establishing a checks and balance on the distribution of these drugs. How can the Baltimore government officials in control of this matter, expect people with severe addiction issues (also many with mental issues as a result of long-term drug use), to be cognizant toward aiding in their own overdose prevention. This is exactly what they are doing by approving Naloxone.

There are Baltimore city police officers, EMT paramedics, and firefighters who are outraged and disgusted by this idea.

Denise Morris

Many believe that these addicts are just going to sell this like they have sold the opiate prescriptions used to help them fight their addiction. Without speculation, a common-sense hypothesis can be proposed on the probability of heroin addicts selling their Naloxone kits. Most of this is mainly because there exist those heroin users who are simply interested in feeding their addiction versus receiving a prescription that aids as a therapeutic and clinical form of treatment. Those individuals are probably elated when drug clinics loosely administer drugs, because those particular addicts' intentions are to use those drugs as collateral or down payment for another type of high.

Baltimore's Drug Crisis and Black Adolescents

There is a serious drug problem and heroin crises in Baltimore. Baltimore city council and policymakers are trying to socioeconomically marginalize and demarcate their means of dealing with the "heroin problem". Considering, the fact that the problem is becoming a "suburbanized" issue, policymakers and Baltimore governing officials are going to be sure to do all that is vested in their power, to redeem white suburban communities. The additional funding for more drug programs and preventative medicine would not be in fruition if white privileged kids were not getting high. Therefore, the aid and funding is marginalized in order to target Baltimore's most valued natives. Meanwhile, drug addicted black adolescents and poor drug addicted white adolescents will probably not benefit from the new up and coming services Baltimore intends to offer to the drug addicted suburban class whites. If this turns out to be the case, Baltimore council members will be guilty the most blatant demonstration of legislative classism and legislative racism. Furthermore, those black adolescents living with drug addicted parents or relatives will significantly be impacted by what Baltimore government intends to offer unto heroin addicted natives. Services provided may be accommodating and may help to revitalize black inner-city families dealing with drug addiction issues.

Drug matters and drug issues should never be racially marginalized and concentrated toward a specific demographic of individuals. Regardless of race, children of all ethnic groups are being groomed, and developed to be future leaders. This task is harder to accomplish in communities that have been aided and coerced (both covertly and overtly) into poverty, by those who hold the lawmaking and policymaking power.

CHAPTER 3

ANALYZING THE SELF-ESTEEM OF BLACK ADOLESCENTS

Definitions and General Characteristics

Merriam-Webster's online dictionary provides a simplistic definition of the word *self-esteem* as a "feeling of satisfaction that someone has in himself and his or her own abilities" (2016). This definition implies that self-esteem arrives from an individual's "contention within". Self- esteem can also be viewed as being happy and confident about your life. A person with high self-esteem often respects their well-being, and the well-being of others.

Need for Study

Self-esteem is essential in daily life because it is a tool that helps us to structure our personal lives. Self-esteem is one of the reasons why morals and values have been established. Morals and values help run the world in a resourceful and organized manner. Morals and values were developed and implemented by individuals with high levels of esteem. The level of esteem these individuals had for themselves, enabled them to develop social mores or customs that allow for others to be considered and treated equally. Self-esteem is not just a part of an individual's psychosocial make-up; it determines how one would most likely socialize him/herself into everyday society. For instance, a person with a high level of esteem, would most likely be outgoing and receptive to human interaction.

How Image and Depiction Affects the Self- Esteem of Young Black Males and Females

When it comes to certain factors that have the ability to affect self-esteem, adolescent African American males and females living in the inner-city face numerous challenges (e.g. poverty, insufficient parenting, broken homes, drug use, incarceration, gang involvement, underage sex, STDs, inferior schooling, etc.). Self-esteem issues can vary for young African American males and females. Young African American males and females may internalize self-esteem differently; depending upon socioenvironmental influences, cultural/family upbringing, and many other associated factors. Furthermore, the depiction of African Americans in social media and/or television also plays a role on how young black girls and young black boys internalize their self-image. Being depicted in the negative via social media implants self-abhorrent thoughts and images of self. Many urbanized black youth spend countless time absorbing these negative depictions of their ethnicity and culture. Most social media and/or television programs either glamorize or paint nefarious stereotypical images of African American males and females. The black male is often sensationalized as a drug dealer, drug addict, thug, negligent father, high school drop-out, and countless other criminalizing images. Saunders et al. (2004) convey African American males have a greater chance of "receiving corporal punishment, to be suspended and to be identified as behaviorally disordered (BD; p.82). Saunders (2004) goes on further to say that young black males are often faced with "isolation and stigmatization". The African American female is almost always sexualized in social media. There exists various television reality shows depicting the black female as a sexual deviant (e.g. whore, prostitute, stripper, unwed mother, etc.). Such demonizing images of both African American males and females behold an invaluable significance as it pertains to self-esteem. When young black males and females are constantly painted in a negative light, they begin to believe that they are a part of a negative and hopeless ethno-cultural background.

Urban black youth in the inner-city are submerged into an environment full of poverty and crime. The educational system in the inner-city are often inferior and lacking the sufficient tools to provide a decent public school education. Therefore, black youth are socialized into an educational climate that may render them cognitively or intellectually underdeveloped or behind in comparison to public schools in economically affluent districts. Urban black youth that are cognizant of these poor educational conditions may ultimately develop a lower self-complex, believing that they are cognitively or developmentally inferior in comparison to other youth that attend better schools.

Subsequently, black youths are at risk for developing low self-esteem when it comes to their academic achievement capabilities. School suffices as a tool to prepare children or scholars for work. If urbanized black youth are constantly faced with inferior schooling, they are also faced with inferior preparation to enter into the workforce to obtain an occupation of their choice. Many may often be discouraged from exploring the possibility of preparing for higher learning at a college institution, because they believe they do not have what it takes to succeed academically.

Lack of academic support and encouragement from outside influences further enhances the risk of lower self-esteem. With no prime examples of success, many urban and poor black youth take the route toward becoming a product of their environment. This means that they would be tempted to resort to crime or immoral acts for economic gain. Jail or death can be one of the devastating outcomes from engaging in criminal activity. Illegal drugs are very prevalent in black urban communities. Drugs are utilized as either a means to "get high" or distribute for economic gain. The byproduct of low self-esteem can either influence drug use or drug dealing. Black youth that have reached this point believe that this is the only way to escape from the ills of life or succeed in their environment. In this case, fractured self-esteem has driven, and convinced the individual that the only way to achieve is by systemically destroying themselves and/or their community.

Denise Morris

Self-Esteem as Interpreted through Abraham Maslow's Hierarchy of Needs Concept

Abraham Maslow's *Hierarchy of Needs* concept can be used to theorize the background of self-esteem as it pertains to black inner-city youth. This hierarchy defines levels of human or basic needs outlined in pyramidal form bottom to top. The most basic needs start at the bottom (e.g. Physiological, Safety, Love/belonging, Esteem, and Self-Actualization). The *Physiological* layer describes the basic instinctual nature of beings: sex/intimacy, competitiveness/dominance, and survival. The *Safety* layer deals with protection/care for health, socio-economic conditions, and mental health. The fourth layer (Love/belonging) focuses on relationships/commitments, family, friends, social life, or the necessity for human interaction. The fifth layer *Esteem* focuses on one's value for self, low/high self-esteem, confidence/lack thereof, and level of self-respect. The last layer pertains to *Self- Actualization*; the responsibility of utilizing your skills to accomplish your goals.

How Hierarchy of Needs Concept Applies to Self- Esteem of Black Female/Male Youth

Most competition is experienced between individuals within the same peer group. Experience usually takes place in social atmospheres (i.e. school, community, social groups, etc.). African American inner-city youth often face conflict in schools.

The drop-out rates are typically higher than black youth from affluent communities with superior schooling institutions. The dropout ratio between black females/males is usually higher for males. There are many vices that could drive both black male and black female out of the institutions of learning. These youths are considered "at risk" because of their social and economic status. At risk means that this sub-culture is more susceptible to incarceration, drug abuse, underage sex, STD exposure, gangs and other risqué associated activity. At risk black youth that struggle with self-esteem issues are more likely to make poor life decisions than those without self-esteem issues.

Furthermore, black inner-city youth are isolated within an environment that suffers from generational perpetuance of social and economic disparity. This means that many black inner-city youth are parented by parents or caretakers that have experienced at least one or more at risk challenges that black inner-city youth face today. Many of these households are single-parented by single black mothers. Lacking the presence of a parent, falls into the category of Maslow's *Love/Belonging* hierarchy of needs concept. This part of the pyramid is associated with one's need and/or yearning for love and support from family, loved-ones, and friends. Self-esteem issues may arise if many inner-city black youths' households are absent of male parents. Many youth may feel or express a sense of neglect from the male parent. This is especially relevant if that male parent is completely absent in his child's life. The child may harbor a strong dislike or resentment toward the absent party due to lack of support. Parental neglect gives a child the perception that the negligent parent does not love or want him/her in their life. Parents are usually the source that teaches the child love and affection. Parents are usually the first ones to care for and nurture their offspring. There is a great chance that a child would experience or feel a lack of self-worth, importance, and purpose. This is likely to effect a child's drive or ambition. Kids with a strong sense of self, come off as very influential and goal-oriented versus kids that do not have a strong sense of self. Those kids with high levels of self-esteem are more likely to be high achievers in life. Kids that exude low self-esteem are more likely to be unsuccessful or run into many obstacles along the way to success.

Summary of Research regarding Black Youth and Self-Esteem

Saunders et al. (2004) conducted a study to determine whether there is a statistically significant "difference in the relationship between self-perceptions and 2 academic outcomes among a sample of 243 African American high school sophomores" (p. 81). Simple random sampling was used to determine why African American females had a greater rate of high school graduation and college enrollment versus African American males. Their hypothesis suggested self-esteem and/or one's self-perception is most likely the cause for the lesser high school graduation rate and college enrollment for African American black males. Saunders et al. (2004) purport "A disparity in educational achievement between males and females has been a persistent trend over the last 2 decades in all racial and ethnic groups in this country" (p. 81). In addition to self-esteem, other variables: "racial self-esteem, academic self-efficacy and importance of school completion to self" (Saunders et al., 2004, p. 82) These other 3 variables were used to predict whether or not 2 independent variables (grade point average and graduation) would be impacted based upon African American female and African American males self-perception. Data was collected using a 7 point *agree/disagree* Rosenberg Self-esteem scale that focused on whether or not the students intended to graduate from high school. Independent paired *t* and bivariate testing was utilized to determine the differences in variable averages between male and female students. Findings were only significant in determining that African American females shown higher levels of self-efficacy than their male counterparts. However, Saunders et al. (2004) maintain that better disciplinary methods must be exercised in the learning environment. They were referring to the school system solely focusing on targeting black male students with harsher disciplinary actions than male student from other ethnic groups.

Prelow et al. (2006) conducted a study to determine whether there is a statistically significant relationship between "ecological risk and depressive symptoms" in urban African

American and European American youth (p. 508). The population consisted of 141 African American high school students and 119 European American high school students. *Competency* was measured utilizing the 7 item Beiser and colleagues competence scale. The reliability coefficients read 0.81 for African American students and 0.83 for European American students (Prelow et al., 2006, p. 511). *Coping Efficacy* was also measured with a 7 item scale "that assessed adolescents' beliefs about their ability to handle problematic situations" (Sandler et al., 2000, Prelow et al., 2006). Coping efficacy reliability coefficients measured 0.74 for African American students and 0.86 for European American students (Prelow et al., 2006). *Self-esteem* was measured with a 10 item Rosenberg Self-esteem scale (Rosenberg, 1965). Questions were agree/disagree in reference to one's own feelings of worth, and the reliability coefficients for self-esteem for African American students and European American students were 0.82 and 0.86 (Prelow et al., 2006). Depressive symptoms were analyzed with the use an altered model of the Center for Epidemiological Studies Depression Scale-Brief Version (CES-D; Roberts and Sobhan, 1992; Prelow et al., 2006). The CES-D measured the following: "*Depressed Affect/Somatic Symptoms, Lack of Well Being, and Interpersonal Difficulties*" the reliability coefficients reflectively of African American to European American youth were 0.80 and 0.77 (Prelow et al., 2006). Hypotheses determined that equally European American and African

American youth presented a greater chance of decreased self-esteem levels and symptomatic depressive features when both ethnic groups were exposed to ecological or environmental risks (Prelow et al., 2006).

The *Rosenberg Self-Esteem Scale* (Rosenberg, 1965), the *Kentucky Inventory of Mindfulness Skill*s (Baer, Smith, & Allen, 2004), and the *Beck Depression Inventory* (Beck & Steer, 1987) were used to conduct a study on a population of 216 undergraduate students, to determine if there is a statistically significant relationship between students' self-esteem and depression. (Michalak et al., 2011). Researchers used the German version of *the Rosenberg Self-Esteem Scale* (Ferring & Filipp, 1996) with a measure of a 0.90 coefficient alpha (Michalak et al., 2011). *The Kentucky Inventory of Mindfulness Skills – accept without judgment subscale* (KIMS-A) is a combinational subscale that includes a 39 item inventory that measures mindfulness and a 9 item subscale to measure non-judgmental behaviors and attitudes towards situations (Michalak et al., 2011). Findings revealed that there is a statistically significant relationship between students' self-esteem and depression. Significance varies based upon the cognitive and emotional stimulation gained from one's own experience. Studies showed that students with strong judgmental attitudes toward their experience most likely viewed a present experience in the negative, and their negative feelings about a situation indicated a susceptibility to depression.

Street et al. (2008) conducted a study that aimed to determine if there is a statistically significant relationship between black adolescents' household environment and mental health as it pertains to influencing ethnic identity. A sample of 61 black adolescents (10- 14 years old) were selected to participate in the study. The study premised around psychologist Erik Erickson's theoretical concept of adolescence and self-identity. *The Family Environment Scale* (FES; Moos and Moos 1994) is the "family conflict and cohesion subscales" utilized to gather quantitative and qualitative data about African American adolescent participants' household structure. The adolescents' Cronbach's alpha reliability coefficients for adolescent, the adolescent's mother, and father's cohesion subscales measured as follows: 0.73 and 0.68; 0.61 and 0.54; and 0.73 with 0.31 cohesion unreliability for the father.

Ethnic identity solidarity was measured by the *Multigroup Ethnic Identity Measure* Likert scale (MEIM; Phinney, 1992), which produced a reliability coefficient of 0.90 (Street et al; 2008). The Behavior Assessment System for Children- Version 2 (BASC-2; Reynolds & Kamphaus, 2004) was the psychometric instrument used to determine the mental health conditions of the black adolescents used in the study. Three keys factors (self-esteem, depression, and interpersonal relationships) were used to measure a series of 31 *true* and *false* questions (Street et al., 2008). The Cronbach's alpha coefficients were 0.78, 0.83, and 0.78 for self-esteem, depression, and interpersonal communication (Street et al., 2008). Results showed that there was a statistically significant relationship between household environment, and mental health in terms of influencing ethnic identity of African American adolescents. Street et al. (2008) conveyed "As predicted, ethnic identity negatively correlated with depression and was positively correlated with self-esteem and interpersonal relationships."

Seaton and Yip (2008) conducted a study on 252 African American adolescents. The study concluded that racial discrimination is more likely to occur when African American youth are placed in diverse academic settings, and diverse neighborhoods where there are only a small percentage of black minorities. Also individual and ethno-cultural racism varies based upon individual perception of racial inequality in the diverse schools and diverse neighborhoods. Findings also revealed that African American female adolescents reported experiencing individual racism at a greater percentage than their male counterparts (Seaton and Yip, 2008). Furthermore, these perceptions had a significant influence on black youth's mental state of health and/or self-esteem levels. A 10 item Rosenberg Self-Esteem Scale (with Cronbach's alpha reliability of 0.85), a 20 item CES-D (with Cronbach's alpha reliability of 0.74), and a 5 item *Satisfaction with Life Scale* (Cronbach's alpha reliability of 0.81) was used to measure self-esteem, depression, and life satisfaction (Seaton and Yip, 2008).

Denise Morris

Seaton (2010) conducted research on 322 African American adolescents to determine whether African American adolescents' "psychological well-being" is statistically and significantly impacted "cognitive development" and "perceived racial discrimination". The ages ranged from 13-18, and 47% were male and 53% were female. *The Phenomenological Variant of Ecological Systems Theory* (PVEST) model was used to analyze the "relationship between perceptions of racial discrimination and psychological well-being among African American youth" (Seaton, 2010). PVEST included questions about the adolescents' age, gender, parent's educational background, individual/cultural racism (Seaton, 2010). Overall, data did determine that cognitive development impacts the mental health and perceptions of racial discrimination (Seaton, 2010). Seaton (2008) further stated that "This finding is consistent with prior research indicating that African American adolescents were more likely to feel victimized by institutional discrimination as opposed to individual discrimination" (Seaton 2008; Fisher et al. 2000).

Prince and Howard (2002) used Abraham Maslow's Hierarchy of Needs to address the issue of fulfilling basic needs of American children. Prince and Howard (2002) analyze the percentage of American children living in poverty to correlate how poverty leads to inferior education, poor learning habits, developmental learning issues, and significant drop out rates. Prince and Howard (2002) also correlated poverty to inferior nutrition, low-income housing, welfare, adolescent pregnancy, criminal activity, and "child abuse" (p. 28). Of Maslow's basic needs, Prince and Howard (2002) go on to mention that unmet physiological needs lead to hunger or infancy death. Malnourishment and starvation through poverty are realities in America. Poverty is also synonymous with Maslow's safety needs. Prince and Howard (2002) make reference to the hazardous and unsafe environmental conditions that impoverished children are faced with. For instance, homes with lead paint are brought up in the discussion. Lead paint is very toxic and studies have shown that it causes cognitive, developmental, physiological, even psychological disorders. These factors interfere with academic achievement and success. Child abuse and neglect can fall under three of Maslow's basic needs (love/belonging, self-esteem, and self-actualization).

A study was conducted on 100 African American young adult females from ages 18-21 to determine if there is a statistically significant relationship between "self-esteem, socio-demographic factors, father-daughter relationships, and sexual risk-taking in an economically diverse group of late-adolescent African American girls" (Peterson, 2007, p. 39). The study is noteworthy, given the statistical facts that African American adolescent females are more susceptible to engage "sexual activity" (Center for Disease Control & Prevention [CDC], 2002; Peterson, 2007). This further increases the risk for sexual transmitted disease and teen pregnancy. Peterson (2008) infers that previous research on the matter "Socio-demographic correlates of sexual risk are often associated with mothers; a trend that may reflect assumptions that fathers are largely absent from their daughters' lives, particularly in low-income families" (Dittus, Jaccard, & Gordon, 1997).

Two psychometric instruments were utilized to conduct this two-part study: *The Sexual History Questionnaire* (Cupitt, 1998), *Taylor's Measure of Self-Esteem* (Taylor & Tomasic, 1996). The Sexual History Questionnaire is a four part, 5 point Likert scale that asks a series of questions regarding sexual activity and sexual behavior. Peterson utilized the Taylor's Measure of Self-Esteem because it measures various aspects of African American women self-esteem on a 16-item scale. Findings from the first study revealed that 25% of the women surveyed were more at risk for contracting a sexually transmitted disease and unplanned pregnancy (Peterson, 2007). Further evidence showed that the educational level of the father is synonymous with African American females sexual risk level. Findings from the second study revealed that fathers' participation in his African American daughters' lives lessens the percentage of sexual risk.

The Outcomes of Healthy Self-Esteem

Research indicates healthy self-esteem is essential for the advancement of African American adolescents; especially, urban African American males and females that live in abstract poverty. Healthy self-esteem is necessary to rise above deplorable socio-economic conditions, to prevent destructive or at risk behaviors, and journey toward a path of success. High self-esteem is reflective of healthy mental hygiene. African American adolescents with low self-esteem are more apt to participate in self-limiting and destructive behavior. Consequently, young African American males are at risk toward becoming another statistic in the criminal juvenile system; adding to the hundreds of thousands of black males that currently populate the United States prison system. Positive experiences and positive environments can help enhance the self-esteem of young black male, and save those at risk. Academic and professional achievement would result verses a life of crime. Young African American females with high self-esteem will be less at risk, when it comes to teenage pregnancy and contracting sexually transmitted diseases. High self-esteem promotes a positive outlook on life. Maintaining a positive outlook on life is essential to urbanized black youth that are socialized in environments plagued with drugs, violence, financial burden, and other debilitating factors that produce a sense of hopelessness. High self-esteem can free African American youth from making poor and unhealthy life choices. Research reveals that low self-esteem places black youth at risk for depression and/or mental disorder. With this being said, self-esteem issues must be addressed in the black community in order to nourish and protect the mental health of black children. These black children are they future; the way that think and feel about their ethnic identity, and individuality can either have a positive or negative impact on their life path.

Why Research is Important in Regards to Self-Esteem and African American Youth

Further research needs to be gathered in order to determine if there is a difference in the way self-esteem impacts African American youth in terms of gender. Data gathered from research articles reveals that most of the self-esteem issues are identical when it comes to African American females and African American males. Most of the research also focuses on urbanized and/or poor black youth. Extensive research is needed to measure the self-esteem levels of black youth from all socio-economic backgrounds. There is no detailed research to determine how middle-class black youth cope with self-esteem issues. There is also need to conduct more studies on black youth that live in affluently diverse communities, where they are a marginalized population versus majority black inner-city population. Studies are scarce as it pertains to how black fathers impact the self-esteem of their black children. A large portion of black youth sampled in various studies, came from single-parented households that were solely parented by the mother. Elaborate analysis of self-esteem from black youth from all social backgrounds is essentially important to offset biases and prevent researchers from making generalizations about black youth and self-esteem.

The provided research has linked low self-esteem to more than at risk behavior. African American female and African American male youth with self-esteem issues, are more susceptible to bouts of depression and social disorders versus those black adolescents without self-esteem issues. Therefore, more research needs to be made available to examine the relationship between black youth self-esteem and depression. This research needs to also expand from a broader demographical perspective, and not limited to black youth that come from a background of poverty and single-parented households.

Literature Review

The Need for Intervention & Research Regarding the Self-Esteem of Black Adolescents

It is essential to address mental health of black females and black males to prevent or lessen the risk of potential mental disorders and/or depression. Failure to address mental health issues in black adolescents increases the risk and their chances of acquiring potential mental disorders in adulthood. The National Alliance on Mental Illness (NAMI, 2016) estimates young American adults ages 18-25 have a 60% chance of suffering from depression than members of the elderly population. NAMI (2016) also convey that suicide is the third cause of death for American teenagers. Although black adolescents are statistically known to have the lowest rate of suicide, they are still more likely to be diagnosed with more complex mental disorders than any other ethnic group. Black adolescent males commit suicide at a higher percentage than their female counterparts, but at a lesser rate than white adolescent males. Black American females in general, have an overall low suicide percentage compared to all other ethnic groups in America. Suicide is the fatal outcome of depression and unaddressed mental health issues. As mentioned, black American females are not committing suicide at such an alarming rate as men and white women. However, black females are most likely to be diagnosed with severe mental illness versus white women.

Such findings present a bias in the mental health profession when it comes to therapy and clinical diagnosis. This bias presents gender and racial inequality as it pertains to minority consumers. An even greater racial disparity is revealed as further findings indicate that black mental health professionals make up only 2% of the mental health workforce (NAMI, 2016). Therefore, most black consumers receive professional mental health treatment from individuals that do not directly identify with their ethno-cultural identity. Lack of black mental health professionals may be the very reason for over-diagnoses of mental illness in black consumers. Such speculations are contingent upon the fact that certain ethnic groups face and/or confront unique issues that are synonymous with their ethnic group. For instance, blacks (especially black males) are more susceptible to racial discrimination and police brutality in America. Black American men are more likely to be incarcerated and given harsher penal sentences than other ethnicities in America. Teenage pregnancy is an issue that black female adolescents face versus white female adolescents.

Black adolescents mental health needs would be best addressed by an experienced professional party that is a part multi-culturally aware or of their own ethnic identity, because these professionals are most likely to share similar life experiences due to similar cultural backgrounds. However, all researchers should take the initiative to become more familiar with the external and internal issues and influences of black adolescents abroad.

A Review of Empirical Research Articles on the Black Adolescents' Self-Esteem Issues

Laar (2000) conducted a study to determine the relationship between black adolescents' low academic achievement and high self-esteem levels. This cross-sectional analysis includes various studies conducted on African American college students to gather information about their self-esteem levels. Laar (2000) makes reference to the academic disparity between black college students as opposed to white college students. Based upon Laar's findings via empirical research, black adolescents go on to college to perform at an inferior academic level compared to white college students. According to Laar's research, there is a significant difference between black and white adolescents when it comes to learning and comprehension. There is an academic "gap" (Laar, 2000) in learning because white adolescent students seem to learn and perform at the level of black students that are 2 or more grad levels above them. For example, a white high school student in his freshmen year may perform at the academic rate of a black high school that is in his/her junior or senior year. These findings were based upon quantitative statistical information gathered from the National Center for Educational Statistics (NCES, 1996), and the American Council on Education (1996). However, much has changed in the last twenty years. African American adolescent girls in the United States are entering into the higher learning institutions in today's society, and they are graduating and achieving at much higher rate than twenty years ago and the civil rights era. Laar (2000) conveys as the academic clock continues to dwindle, so does the scholastic prowess and interest of aging black students. Laar then acknowledges that college enrollment increased significantly between the mid-70s and mid-80s. These findings were based upon the statistical data collected by Higher Education and National Affairs (1986), which stated that 40% of black in the United States were entering institutions of higher learning at a higher rate than ever before. On the contrary, Laar emphasizes the disproportionate college graduate rates amongst black college students and white college students. Besides poor academic achievement, Laar mentions affordability and lack of financial aid are also reasons for the lesser percentage of college enrollment of black as compared white college student enrollment. Whites' ability to continue to afford college in spite of the consistent rising cost of tuition illustrates that there is still social-economic disparity nearly two decades later. Lower levels of academic achievement in black students at the college level can very well be due to the social-economic disparities faced on the elementary and secondary school level, because lower income students are usually placed in poor quality schools with inferior education material. It is well known that poverty and limited education will hinder any youth from exceling academically, when faced with these debilitating circumstances.

Black Students Self-Esteem vs. Academic Excellence

Laar's research was conducted in contrast with discouraging research that hypothesized the educational underachievement of black students would be a great hindrance to their performance at higher learning institutions. These studies further hypothesized that lower academic achievement would deter blacks from even attempting to pursue a college education. Laar was able to purport that researchers that conducted the studies on black students' self-esteem came up with surprising results that countered their predictions. Studies conducted revealed that black students' self-esteem levels with either above or equal to the self-esteem levels of white students.

Laar (2000) utilized the Weiner's attribution theory of motivation and emotion (Weiner, 1986, 1992) to analyze the self-esteem of African American students from previous empirical research collected from various studies. Weiner's attribution theory is comprised of two models: the self-esteem model that focuses on self-esteem and productively, and the external model that concentrates on "internal attributions for their lower outcomes" (Laar, 2000). Qualitative data gathered from the self-esteem model indicated African American students' low self-esteem/low academic achievement is most likely because of their social influences, and environment. In other words, African American students' depiction of their ethnocultural makeup, socioeconomic status, and quality of living is indicative of their levels of achievement. The external model helped researchers determine that African American students' self-esteem appeared higher because their internal levels of low self-esteem and poor academic achievement influenced them to focus solely on their exterior or physical appearance. In essence, the selected population of African American students, masked their underachievement through materialism.

Adult Influence in Black and White Adolescents' Lives

Hirsch et al. (2002) conducted a study to determine if there is a statistically significant difference how adult influence impacts black adolescents versus white adolescents. A total of 122 high school students ranging from ages 14-19 years of age were selected based upon gender and race. The causal-comparative research study utilized the parametric statistical multivariate analysis of variance (MANOVA) to gather statistical data on the basis of race and gender.

Parental background, family, and culture were three factors used to measure how adult influence impacted both black adolescents and white adolescents. Black mothers had a significantly lower percentage of higher education compared to white mothers. ANOVA testing was conducted to determine the socioeconomic status of black student participants' parents versus the socioeconomic status of white student participants' parents. Results determined that the black families grossed lesser income than white families. However, one-parent homes had lesser incomes overall, regardless of race.

Hirsch et al. (2002) obtained nominal data from the student participants. A nominal questionnaire was given; asking students which grandparent (male or female) was most influential in their lives. Furthermore, a 3-item scale was used to measure black adolescent and white adolescent male and female growth level, relationship with parent, and peer relationships (Hirsch et al., 2002). A 6-point Likert scale utilized to measure adolescent growth which revealed a Cronbach's Alpha reliability measure of .78 and .73 for both grandparent and prominent influential adult male (Hirsch et al., 2002). In comparison, the Cronbach's alpha ratio measures were .91 grandparents and .87 the

Denise Morris

prominent adult male influence upon adolescent and parent relationships. Each adult Cronbach Alpha reliability measured .87 when it came to their influence on adolescents peer relationships.

Hirsch et al. (2002) research determined that the maternal grandmother had a greater influence (60 percent) upon their teenage grandchildren. The adult male (non-parent) had a 44 percent influence over adolescents, and grandfathers' were favored 52 percent by white male adolescent participants (Hirsch et al., 2002). Overall, 70 percent black adolescent participants were more than likely to identify their grandmother as the most influential adult figure. Research also revealed that black females found greater influences in non-parent and/or non-familial adults. White adolescent males were more likely to identify with an influential adult male figure than their counterparts.

Researchers further convey that divorce and single parent households could be why many adolescent participants strongly identify with the female grandparent, because grandparents are usually involved in the upbringing of the child when to assist the single parent. Therefore, family structure has a significant impact on what adult figure may be most influential in the child's life. Culturally, female figures are very significant in the lives of black adolescents. Especially in the inner-city communities. This is because there are significantly more maternal single-parent black households within the inner-city. The mothers of the single-parent mothers often step in and assist in the rearing of the child. These grandmothers take on the role as childcare provider, nurturer, and mentor. It is not unusual to find many black adolescents living with their grandparents. Black grandparents often take guardianship of the child if the parent is unable or deceased. Usually, it is the black grandmother who steps up and takes on the responsibility of the mother or father parent. This is why black children usually gives thanks to their grandmothers when they achieve certain levels of success. Many of this can be seen from black athletes and/or entertainers that have reached superstardom. In many ceremonial events, the black child usually pays homage to either mother or grandmother. This is because black single-parent household are usually matriarchal versus patriarchal. So it is only natural that the black adolescent would display more adulation toward the female adult in his/her life on a consistent basis.

Intervention to Prevent African American Male Incarceration

Okwumabua et al. (1999) implemented an interventional study to decrease the ratio of African American adolescent male incarceration. The study emanated from the statistical facts provided by the West Tennessee Juvenile Court Report on African American adolescent male imprisonment. Statistics revealed that black males in America were most likely to be imprisoned at a much higher rate than any other race of male adolescents.

A total of 122 black adolescent males within the age range 8-14 were selected from four West Tennessee public schools to participate in the study (Okwumabua et al., 1999). A 10 item Stephan-Rosenfield Racial Attitude Scale [SRAS] (Stephan & Rosenfield, 1979) and a 10 item Banks Attitude Scale [BAS] (Banks, 1984) were used to assess students' racial attitude and level of self-esteem..." (Okwumabua et al., 1999). Both scales are of a Likert type. Before starting intervention, researchers utilized the Center for Disease Control and Prevention (CDC) Decision-Making Instrument (CDC, 1984) to determine the black adolescent male participants' ability to make decisions. Decision-making skills, conflict resolution skills, and cultural awareness were the invention variables used in the study. Participants were required to attend 50 minute sessions of intervention for nearly a year (Okwumabua et al., 1999). Intervention involved activities to improve self-esteem levels and cultural education, to teach the black adolescent male participants the significance of their ethnocultural history. This study is an experimental research design that aimed to transform the cognitive behavior of the selected subjects in hopes to deter violent behavioral patterns that ultimately result in disciplinary action and/or imprisonment.

Findings indicate black adolescent male participants displayed conflicting feelings toward their environment.

Findings also shown that temperament of the social climate is most likely the cause for violent behavior in black adolescent males. For instance, black males from hostile communities may be more susceptible to display aggressive or violent behavior. The intervention provided no real remedy to reduce the incarceration of black males. However, the self-esteem of the black males did increase as indicated in post studies. Perhaps increased self-esteem coupled with cultural awareness can promote healthy behavioral skills as long as the subject values his being and his African American heritage.

Preventive Intervention for African American Youth

Okeke-Adeyanju et al. (2014) conducted a study to determine if intervention would help impact black adolescents' self-esteem, parent- child communication, and racial identity. The intervention was a program called Celebrating Strengths of Black Youth (CSBY), and a group of black youth ages 7-10 were randomly recruited to partake in the study (Okeke-Adeyanju et al., 2014). The experimental study consisted of 10 session group meeting to enhance the self-esteem of the participants. The study allowed the parental attendance in 3 out of the 10 sessions (Okeke-Adeyanju et al., 2014). There was a control that were on a waiting list to partake in the CSBY program. Results revealed black youth that participated in the program showed higher levels of self-esteem than the group that did not attend. A combination of parametric statistic testing was performed to

47

measure the statistical significance of the intervention. Researchers also considered the demographical variables of the black adolescent participants to gain a broader perspective of how such factors would influence intervention prevention. The Behavioral Assessment System for Children, 2nd edition (BASC-2; Reynolds & Kamphaus, 2004) instrument was utilized in the study to determine if the participants had certain behavioral problems (Okeke-Adeyanju et al., 2014)

Research suggest black youth faced with constant discrimination are at risk for lower self-esteem. Discrimination upon the basis of ethnic identity, causes many black adolescents to create false and negative perceptions of self. Racial stigmas and stereotypes bestowed upon black youths are synonymous with and contributory toward the diminishing of their self-enhancement and social skills. Black youth become ostracized and alienated within society, when racial stigmas and stereotypes depict them as villains and/or menaces to society. Okeke-Adeyanju et al. (2014) imply "Racial socialization is the process by which society transmits messages to youth about the significance and meaning of their race..." (p. 358). Furthermore, decreased self-esteem levels can be linked to some black adolescents' poor academic achievement, and lack of interpersonal activity.

Intervention Concerning Adolescent Females Health and Self- Image

LeCroy (2004) conducted an experimental preventive intervention study to examine young adolescent females' psychosocial health. A total of 118 young middle school adolescent girls were selected and divided into two separate groups (59 controlled group and 59 treatment group; LeCroy, 2004). The adolescent females where of white, African American, Native American, and Hispanic descent. Information was primarily obtained through self-reports. The intervention was called Go Grrrls, and geared toward "being a girl in today's society, establishing a positive self-image, establishing independence, making and keeping friends, learning to obtain help and find access to resources, and planning for the future" (LeCroy, 2004).

This study focused on the ways young adolescent females view themselves, and the way media portrays an archetypal image for females' measure to in order to win the approval American's "popular culture". Therefore, one goal of the intervention was to help these young adolescent girls to actualize and define their own image. LeCroy (2004) made mention about society being more focused and obsessed over the females' external layer, and clinicians being more concerned because measuring up to such standards can be depressing and overwhelming for adolescent females. Findings shown that "body image" (LeCroy, 2004) seemed to be a solid focal point, because "From a cultural perspective body image is what often has negative and long lasting impact for girls" (p. 467).

This study has its limitations from an ethnocultural perspective. For instance, the researcher admits that less than 2 percent of African American females were selected. This comprises internal validity to a degree because studies were conducted in a geographical area where the prevalence of blacks is null. Therefore, the researcher could not get an adequate analysis of how African American females are impacted by self-image stigmatizations. Furthermore, there were no stabilizing variables to illustrate how African American females, and other minority females in America feel about television and social media's constant attempt to define female beauty from a Eurocentric viewpoint.

Intervention for Crime Offending Black Adolescent Males vs. White Adolescent Males

As stated previously, *at risk* black adolescent males are more susceptible to being involved in criminal activity as either victim or initiator. This is mainly because of ecological circumstances of impoverishment. Neighborhood or community issues have a great impact upon male adolescents off all walks of life. However, black adolescents with low self-esteem are at greater risk to participate in risqué behaviors that lead to disciplinary action or life threatening experiences.

A total of 625 adolescent males (equal selection of black adolescent males and white adolescent males) participated in a two-part longitudinal study (Buffalo Longitudinal Study of Young Men [BLSYM]) for the purposes of gathering data about criminal activity and victimization and "offending amongst youth" to determine "various neighborhood risk factors" (Hartinger- Saunders et al., 2012). Information was gathered by self- reporting surveys that asked a series of questions about neighborhood crime and neighborhood safety.

Researcher's purported that black adolescent males with low socioeconomic status (SES) experienced victimization and neighborhood crime at higher levels than black adolescent males with higher SES, and white adolescent males (Hartinger-Saunders et al., 2012). Hartinger- Saunders et al. (2012) used "The Chi-Square, Comparative fit index (CFI), the Tucker-Lewis fit index (TLI), the root mean square error of approximation (RMSEA), and weighted room mean square residual (WRMR)" instruments to analyze data and information gathered from the study.

Findings revealed that property crimes where the most reported crimes experienced in the participants' neighborhoods. This was not generally an expected outcome. Especially for communities with low SES. More than half of the selected group reported being victims of property crimes (Hartinger- Saunders et al., 2012). Property theft and/or property crime does not seem as surprising as being one of the most committed neighborhood crimes. This is because theft is most likely to be a way for poor criminals to acquire valuables that they cannot afford. Research continues to prove that poverty has a statistically significant impact upon adolescents regardless of ethnicity or gender. Poverty is a social and economic condition that ecologically welcomes crimes like illegal drug trafficking, violence, gangs, assaults, and all other related conditions that systematically degrade a community. It is not uncommon for impoverished adolescents to become products of their environment; especially, when there are no positive adult figures within their lives.

Intervention Research Findings from Non- American Study on Adolescent Self- Esteem

It is necessary to get a global perspective of adolescents' self-esteem in order to determine if there are common patterns that influences self- esteem levels. Although, the premise of this research is to examine the self- esteem levels of African American adolescent males and African adolescent males, broader comparisons must be drawn from a statistical point of view, to understand how adolescent self- esteem issues are relative as opposed to marginal on the basis of social demographics such as income and skin color.

Delinquent Behavior and Correlational Effects on Adolescents

Mann et al. (2014) purport:

Peer deviance is a robust contextual correlate of adolescents'delinquent behavior (Kandel, 1986), an association that reflects social selection and social influence (Burk, Vorst, Kerr, & Stattin, 2011; Wills & Cleary, 1999). Social selection is a process by which adolescents with dispositions toward delinquency select (and are selected into) deviant peer groups (Gottfredson & Hirsch, 1990; Kandel, 1978). (p. 129)

This information, suggests delinquent behavior is synonymous to the adolescents environmental and/or social climate. Such findings further emphasize adolescent females and adolescent males that struggle with self-esteem, are more susceptible to engage in delinquent behavior if the social atmosphere presents the elements that promote social deviancy. An inference can also be made about black adolescent youth that struggle with low self- esteem and poverty.

A study was conducted to determine the statistically significant relationship between adolescents social environment and "adolescent delinquency" Mann et al. (2015). This study is known as the Texas Twin Project because a population of 470 twins ages 13-17, were selected to participate in the study (Harden et al., 2013). Males outnumbered the adolescent female participants by four-percent. Majority of the participants were white adolescents (58%), then Hispanic (21%), African American (11%), and an even smaller percentage of all other considered minority adolescents (Mann et al., 2015). A 36- item self-reporting questionnaire, pertaining to adolescent delinquent behavior, was used as a psychometric instrument to gather and analyze quantitative data on the selected participants. A 3-point scale was used to measure the parents' monitoring skills and knowledge of their child's social activity.

One result included that delinquent adolescents who strongly demonstrate at risk behavior characteristics often attach to other delinquent peers. These findings can be helpful toward understanding how perpetuated poverty perpetuates delinquent black communities, and how these factors contribute to the decline of self-esteem in black adolescents: these factors ultimately create detrimental outcomes for black adolescents who choose to associate themselves with delinquent and/or criminal behavior. Furthermore, the self-esteem of black adolescents' are further jeopardized if their social environment is negative, and dysfunctional.

Purpose of Study

The purpose of this study was to determine if there is a statistically significant difference in self- esteem levels of African American adolescent females and African American adolescent males. Empirical data has been provided to gather statistical outcomes of certain factors influential to the self-esteem of black adolescents. Analytical research draws various conclusions regarding a myriad of self-esteem concerns as it pertains to black adolescents.

Significance of the Study

Such research is important, due to the fact that there is not enough information of empirical content, which analyzes the effects low self-esteem has on black youth. Most empirical research presents an ethnic bias, which reveals researchers' contingency upon focusing on mental health issues solely from the perspective of the affluently white majority. There is little valid research on the mental health matters as it pertains to blacks and other minorities in general. Furthermore, adolescent health is important regardless of race; however, racial inequality and socioeconomic barriers between black and white adolescents need to prompt researchers to approach research on black adolescents accordingly.

Understanding the mental health needs of African American adolescents can contribute towards determining possible prevention intervention methods to enhance the self-esteem levels of black adolescent males and black adolescent females. Research conducted upon the basis of varying ecological black communities, and socioeconomic statuses can provide, data and information about the differences and/or similarities of self-esteem issues between black adolescents from different social demographical backgrounds.

Global comparative studies are also necessary to determine if there is a statistically significant difference between the self-esteem issues, and self-esteem levels of non- African American black adolescents in other countries outside of the United States.

Denise Morris

This is important towards determining if there is link between the ways black adolescents cope with self-esteem issues. This will also reveal any racial inequality in non- American empirical studies as it pertains to black mental issues. It is imperative to determine whether the nature of black adolescents' self-esteem is impacted more negatively or positivity based upon geographical climate.

Do black adolescents in Europe face different circumstances influencing self-esteem than black American adolescents? Are there more prevention intervention strategies implored to influence black adolescent self-esteem in non- American countries? Are factors such as racism, low SES, and poverty as damaging to black adolescents self-esteem in other countries than in America? Are black mental health needs excluded and/or poorly studied by researchers in countries abroad as it is in America? These are considerable questions that can enhance the study of black mental health. Most empirical research on the matter of black self-esteem have drawn the same conclusions on black adolescents' self-esteem: poverty and crime are the most common influences on the self-esteem levels of black adolescents, single parent households or weak family structures, and degenerate ecological social settings. Researchers' findings must delve beyond the range of reducing black adolescents' self-esteem outcomes to familial structures, and the black communities in which dwell. While this information is statistically proven in many case studies of black self-esteem, it is not determinate of all conditions responsible for influencing black adolescents' self-esteem.

CHAPTER 4

EXAMINING URBAN BLACK COMMUNITY STRUCTURES

The urban black familial structure must first be explored before examining black community structures. Organically, families are what makes communities or neighborhoods. In a community, families can be nuclear (consisting of two-parent household), families are also single-parent, and extended or blended (a combination of both nuclear and single-parent, with elderly generational families members such as grandparents, aunts, and/or uncles). The black inner-city family structure has a higher percentage of single-parent household. As mentioned in the previous chapter, most of these households are of a matriarchal structure or parented by the black mother. This means that she is the only parent in the household that provides for the welfare of her offspring.

One party income is one disadvantage of the single-parent household. Some single parents may receive court ordered child support. In many cases, black inner-city single-parent mothers do not receive court ordered child support from the male parent. Other cases, the father may not live in the household but equally support his offspring. More severe circumstances concerning single-parenting in the inner-city involve total neglect and absence from the father.

It is not uncommon that many inner-city males father multiple children by multiple women. The hardship and burden often falls on the female parent; and she is most likely to have to face the economic responsibility alone. This is especially if the father has multiple other children and has proven to be a serial deadbeat parent. Other destabilizing factors or disadvantages are incarceration of the male parent, drug addiction, preoccupation with criminal activities, and/or death. While these outcomes can exist in any social class or race, it favors and is an ingredient in the inner-city because the prevalence of poverty produce such systematic outcomes.

Social-Economic Disadvantages in Baltimore's Inner-City

The truth of social-economic disparity is self-evident within the inner-city setting. According to US Census Bureau (2013) a reported 37% of black men between age ranges 20-24 are unemployed in the city of Baltimore. In hindsight, one would assume that the possibility of employment is more likely for black men of Baltimore City, because the city of Baltimore is 63% black or African American. Lack of work experience, insufficient education, criminal activity, and incarceration are the usual contributing factors and reasons for over a one-third of young black males' statistically significant unemployment rate. This rate is nearly four times higher than their white male counterparts. The black male demographic sets a portion of the economic tenor in the inner-city community of Baltimore. As a current resident living in Baltimore city's uptown area, I can say that it is not uncommon to witness unemployed black males between the ages of 18-25 wondering the streets all hours of the day, loitering, openly smoking marijuana, selling illegal goods, selling illegal drugs, or panhandling. This does not apply to all of the 37% of unemployed black males or those of the 37% that may be unemployed for totally legitimate circumstances. Neither can these numbers reveal occupational discrimination on the bases of race, lack of employment opportunities available within the city, and temporary job assignments.

The numbers do reveal there is a real problem and imbalance of occupation for young black adult males than young white adult males. One is left to consider whether or not there is a phobia of black inner-city men who are young adults. The evidence can be seen each time I travel to affluent Baltimore city districts such as Midtown, Canton, Fells Point, Locus Point, and Federal Hill. The retail and food and beverage businesses begin to look whiter than anything. Black employees within these environments become scarce or are in the background (i.e. kitchens, stockrooms, outdoors), away from clientele. Meanwhile, there are many blacks that consume products from businesses in the grander scale neighborhoods in the city.

Black Women's Economic Status in the Community

The black woman is the most contributive force within the community. Her money, rather scarce or sufficient, travels far within her community. The black woman contributes and dishes out a higher amount of revenue as an American consumer verses all other consumers from various social demographical backgrounds. According to the Neilson Company (2013), black women in the US consumer expenses generate well over 1 trillion dollars. Such findings are somewhat of an economic anomaly, considering that black women earn less than males and white females. Whether high or low socioeconomic status (SES), black women's purse power influences the economic growth of this country on a grander scale than men, and women of other ethnicities. According to the ending of the 2015 fiscal year (FY15), the gross national debt is 18.1 trillion dollars. The spending power of black women equals more than 10% of that debt. This fact is another finding that is an anomaly; considering the way media tries to portray black women as the posterchildren of welfare, and the most destitute women upon the planet. As black women, we benefit the free-market economy to a degree that the economy would nearly collapse or face a huge economic setback, if we took just one day off from spending.

This information makes it hard to conceive many black women are still living in poverty at a mass ratio. Usually, the urban ghetto is most likely the inner-city. Author, lecturer, and film director, Tariq Nasheed (2016) refers to black ghettos as "concentration camps". By definition a concentration camp is where a race, class, or certain group of people are placed (usually by the government or ruling class) into disadvantage conditions that limit or negate their ability to rise socially, economically, politically, and in any other way that advances the well-being of a people. Tariq Nasheed is dead on with his depiction of black inner-city communities. Most black inner-city communities', by nature, structure, and socioeconomic conditions are concentration camps. The criteria of the black ghetto fits the definition and eclipses the meaning with such perfect balance. This is most definitely a design and well planned agenda enforced by governing bodies, to keep blacks, (especially black women), at a certain level of inferiority and subservience.

Many inner-city black women purchase exclusively within their neighborhoods or nearby neighboring areas. The black woman's dollar goes from anywhere to grocery stores, restaurants, clothing stores, health clinics/medical centers, childcare providers/daycare, church/community associations, housing, and schooling. Subsequently, black women within inner-city are usually the breadwinners or head-of-household. More than 70% of black households in the black community consist of black single parent mothers. It is amazing how black women across America persevere, regardless of a seemingly conspired and coerced socioeconomic disposition. It is because of this the black woman is often stigmatized as a matriarch or black male loathing bitter black woman. The black woman is often blamed for systematic conditions rendered before her. Such conditions were orchestrated before her conception and already set into play during the arrival of our African ancestors by way of the Middle Passage. Yes, slavery is still an existing condition that is more covert and masked, through the limited liberties and freedoms we're entitled to receive, due to our 14th Amendment rights. The social disregard of the black woman is a primary example and confirmation of the present existence of slavery.

The family structure in the inner-city is extended due to the mass proportion of single-parent households. Contrary to the media's emphasis on black on black crime and negative stereotyping of the black family; black inner-city families often combine their resources to help one another. As mentioned in earlier chapters, grandparents, aunts, uncles, cousins, may assist one another with raising children, paying living expenses, and other related situations. The extended black family is the true definition of welfare and social reform. They come together to ensure the quality and welfare of the other. I am the product of an extended family. I have benefited from extended loved ones in so many ways (i.e. socioeconomically, spiritually, emotionally, academically, etc.). The black extended family in the inner-city are one of the most valuable types of family structures. This is mainly because of abundance of support, guidance, and love.

Denise Morris

Value and Importance of Black Family Structure

One day, I engaged in a very powerful and exhilarating conversation with a well-educated West Indian black brother, as I dined in St. Mary's (a renowned Jamaica restaurant in Baltimore City's Charles Village district). Our conversation set up the platform for me to discuss this very book (*Rage in Baltimore*). He asked, "Which family structure is more important." I thought long and hard about the question he posed. I considered his background as a Jamaica native born into a single-parent household. I considered the fact of him being black Caribbean male child raised only by a female parent, and an absent father. I considered the fact that absent black fathers in the black household seems to be a globalized epidemic, and not just a geographically exclusive condition and experience of black American children. It is also a prime example of how the William Lynch, slave master, divide and conquer tactic worked on folks of African descent.

Africans were brought through the Caribbean islands to be "conditioned" or seasoned into slavery. The breaking of the African took place solely in the Caribbean before the African was shipped off elsewhere in America, to endure a harsh life as free labor workhorse, deemed three-fifths of a human being for property and insurance purposes. Chattel is the traditional name used when referencing the African slave. During the seasoning of our ancestors, many were estranged and separated from their spouses and children. Slavery is the root and primary reason for the perpetuation of absent black fathers in America. Black men had already been conditioned through slavery, to be misplaced, relocated against their will, and estranged from their significant others and children.

Slavery of the African in America is also responsible for the lack of family structure and the stereotyped virility and promiscuity of the black man and the black woman. This is because Anglo Saxon white male supremacist slave master's bred the black male and black female. This means the white slave master's coerced the African slaves to engage in sex (regardless of their familial relationship or lack thereof) in order to produce more offspring to aid in the free labor market economy of slavery. In addition to breeding, the African slave (both male and female) endured sexual abuse at the hands of their slave masters. It was not unusual for a slave master to advance himself sexually upon a female slave of his choice and desires. This means he would either bribe or rape his female slave. Bribery was just a thing to soothe the white slave master's immoral disposition, because he had the right to do whatever to his slave. The slave was considered subhuman and property. A person can do what they please with their prized possessions. The slave master did just as he pleased. African male slaves were raped as well. Miscegenation or mulattoes originated from slavery. A mulatto child on the plantation revealed the slave master's infidelity to his white wife, and his mishandling of his slaves. Although the slave master's wife was conditioned to despise the African slave as an inferior species, she was well aware that African slave was very much human, and a woman with the same lady parts as her. Most importantly, she became aware that her husband was a thief, philanderer, rapist, and pimp.

It is no wonder why quite a few black males living the rapper or entertainer lifestyle, refer to themselves as pimps, hustlers, and gangsters. The DNA of the African slave ancestors' captors flows through the bloodstream of our children in these modern day times. Many black greater grandparents speak of having a white father or grandfather. Once again, that is the evidence of the raping of our ancestors through the auspice of slavery.

Is the Black Inner-City the New Plantation?
The city of Baltimore is filled with neighborhoods that unapologetically intersect and merge. This means neighborhoods of squalor and abstract poverty, eclipse the affluent and well-to-do neighborhoods. One would assume this would be a grave problem to have, the impoverished co-existing with the socioeconomically astute citizens of Baltimore's city. However, this is not the case. In fact, many of the impoverished keep crime inclusive within their environment. The police presence is also there to ensure this type of social order. The cops stake out in the inner-city where the predominant blacks are and stand guard. The cops perform hourly patrols in the affluent neighborhoods, making sure nothing is out of place, for the sake of ensuring the

quality of their high tax bracket citizens of the city who are predominantly white.

It would amaze the average tourist or non-resident to see projects or Section 8 housing, directly around the corner or across the street from some of the most prestigious, and wealthiest housing and architecture that Baltimore city has to offer. By design, majority of these projects are housed by low-income and/or poor blacks. The projects are intentionally set up like death traps; one way in and one way out, with little to no nighttime lighting for visibility. It's no wonder why they never seem to clearly identify suspects who may have committed a crime in the projects. Many of the project complexes are filthy, poorly maintained with unreliable and inconsistent housing. One would assume, the city would take more pride in the communities they house.

The projects are very much synonymous to a slave plantation. Socially and economically, the inhabitants of the housing projects are in a predicament of extreme despair. They are crowded and cramped together, as our black enslaved ancestors were, when they slept in the shanty slave quarters. Cops pretend to patrol the housing project areas. Most of the time you can see them on their phones or iPads, completely and intentionally clueless to the numerous drug transactions occurring right under their noses. The white slave-master that owned the plantation, surveyed his black field servants, to make sure they did not step out of line or slack off on the field work. Often times, the white slave master would get another field slave to oversee the plantation work, and crack the whip upon the back of any field hand that did not obey his master's order. In the projects of Baltimore, the police is that field hand. Their objectives are not prevent crime to ensure the safety of the inhabitants in project housing. Baltimore City police job is to make sure the social dysfunction and chaos remains exclusively within the projects, where the poor blacks live. You will be approached or targeted, if you wander off into the more affluent parts, and the cops perceive you as a recipient of rundown black inner-city neighborhoods. They are not afraid to crack the whip or nightstick when it comes to handling our troubled inner-city black youth. The death of Freddie Gray, is prime example of how far Baltimore cops would go to keep social order.

There have several times where a Baltimore City cop has pulled me over for some made up reason, runs my license and registration, and then allowed me to proceed on my way. Most of these times, I was within my neighborhood either coming from work or school. These cops were definitely profiling me. If you are black, and live in a nice section of the neighborhood, some cops assume you do not belong there, and you are probably there to commit a crime. Usually, the white cops do this because they have no multicultural training and understanding of black inner-city communities. Many of them are from small white towns where black were scarce. Many become cops, working a beat amongst black inhabitants, and perceive all blacks as some sort of threat. It is impossible to take a bunch of white cops like this serious, because they are mostly xenophobes with white supremacist ideological thinking; many were raised to feel and think this way about blacks. These are mainly the types to be trigger happy, when they encounter what they perceive to be an unruly Negro. White racist cops tasked with patrolling any black neighborhood is a toxic and dangerous because they do not care for the well-being of blacks. Therefore, whatever crimes black commit amongst themselves is justifiable and acceptable to these white racist cops in Baltimore. The racist white cops believe it makes their job easier when black kill another. Black on black violence is also synonymous to being a black slave overseer on the plantation, cracking the whip on your black brothers and sisters.

There is a lot of social disconnect between inner-city black in Baltimore. The young adult inner-city black males are the main group responsible for majority of inner-city homicides among blacks. As always, the news broadcast it as a "potential" drug or gang related incident (which is not always the case). The media must also play its part to reinforce the negative stereotypes about Baltimore's black inner-city communities. The perception is always every black person in Baltimore's inner-city is on some type of drugs or into criminal activity.

Denise Morris

Summing Up the Community Structural Design

Demographically and statistically, the black inner-city of Baltimore (as many black inner-cities designed by the government, to create pre-existing familial conditions meant to disadvantage the black community) largely consist of black mother single-parented households, black elderly homeowners (who are long-term residents), a large number of young black men who are unemployed, or black men absent from the community do to incarceration.

The stronghold within the community are usually the single-parenting black mothers, her family, and the elderly. Many of the inner-city elderly aid in caring for their children's children or some other relatives children. Their assistance benefits the inner-city community socioeconomically, spiritually, and historically. They are the plethora of knowledge and truly understand how our inner-city community got into this present condition. They are the long-term and upstanding members of the community. The elderly understand that we have been conspired against, others of us have willingly participated in the decline of our own neighborhoods, and the black inner-city has had its share of victims and victimizers.

Recapturing the question posed to me: *What family structure counts the most?* Quite frankly, each structure is of importance. The old saying goes *'it takes a village to raise a child'*. Most importantly, stability is what it takes to make any family setting successful. Many argue the two-parent household argument. The more parental influence, the more guidance, and diversity of experience enhances positive outcomes. However, if one parent is leading a positively influential example, and the other the opposite, there lies social disorder within that household. Usually, troubled children are products of disorderly environments, the first experience of environment is the household. There is a greater possibility that children living in this environment will demonstrate disorderly behaviors, because of the polarity of parental guidance or structure. One parent is doing whatever it takes to while the other is destroying the foundation of a stable family structure.

These contrasting environments leak out into the inner-city, painting an abstract portrait which signifies so many different social outcomes and expectancies. The children are the conduits that watch and observe to a tea, the happenings within their community. They absorb and filter in the knowledge, the non-sense, along with the mental and spiritual blessings, and poisons. They copy, trace, recall, and mimic the verbal and non-verbal patterns of behavior. They adapt and adopt language of their environment to venture off to other environments (i.e. schools, affluent communities, workforce/corporate structures, legal system, etc.) to either be accepted or rejected as other (black minority). A black child growing up in the inner-cities, whether Baltimore or other inner-cities in the US, realizes how much he/she is targeted and ostracized at an early stage in their adolescence. They acknowledge this inclusively within their own community, socially, amongst their peer groups and households. Many black inner-city adolescents experience their first form of police harassment before they're adults, because they are socialized as delinquents of society. They're misunderstood and misdiagnosed as hyperactive in the schooling system, and revered by non-black (even some black) educators who are out of touch with their cultural make-up.

These very reasons are why a strong black community is essential to our youth. It does not matter if the family structure is nuclear, single-parent, or extended. Regardless, strong and proficient households, set the tone for an even equal type of community. As a black community, we must pool together and challenge the way our local, state, and government officials overlook our residents. We are entitled to the same luxuries, privileges, and happiness enjoyed by those Baltimoreans (white majority of social and economic affluence) on the outskirts of the city. Our children shall not be vilified in our neighborhood public schooling systems. They are socialized as criminals in our local public schools. Several Baltimore city public schools have metal detector to inspect our children like inmates before entering the school campus. This type of administrative authority subliminally and demonstratively conditions our children (especially our male children who are targeting by school administrators) to accept prison state conditions and environments. Subsequently, it prepares them for jail. Meanwhile, several public schools and universities of majority white-privileged communities where mass school shootings have occurred, have yet to enforce metal detectors or a strong police presence in their schooling districts. This is because we're stuck in a system that enforces white supremacy, and the oppression of blacks, other people of color; those considered "minorities". The control is obvious when we associate words such as minority and majority to ethnicity (black/white). However, as black individuals, we must fight hard to instill value in our youth as the odds are intentionally and thickly against them.

Denise Morris

CHAPTER 5

The Impact of Black Male Incarceration in Baltimore

Black male incarceration is the highest in the United States. Judicial disparity, under the auspices of race and white patriarchal male supremacy, has allowed for a legislative, executive, and judicial system that intentionally and predatorily target black males. In addition to the racial inequality exercised through the legal system, socioeconomically, corporations (mainly private industries) in America profit off of the hands of free labor provided by inmates (inmates that are majority black male prisoners).

The Bureau of Justice (2013) documented nearly 800,000 black men are incarcerated in the US. This is alarming considering blacks as a whole, make up about 13% (46 million) of the population. This is a form of covert slavery that functions under the false pretenses of solely maintaining social order and moral uniformity. While there are black males that are repeat offenders and belong in jail, there are also the unfair laws that segregate certain crimes that are considered "black" and impose harsher penalties upon those who commit them. There are many black men serving *hard time* (long prison sentences) for petty offenses or non-violent crimes. Meanwhile, there are others serving time for crimes that they physically had no involvement in; there are others who are serving crime for conspiring. One can clearly see that the role of the US judicial system is to try and persecute the black man as defending party. There is essentially no safe place for a black man who chooses to operate above or outside the law. Institutionalized racism and slavery have set the tenor to make the plight of the male a turbulent one. Therefore, any black male who betrays the moral code of the US democracy is skating on thin ice. He is flirting and defying laws which have never been designed to protect him or his loved ones. There is no way that the Constitution of the United States sought to protect blacks when it was written during an era of when many (including our founding fathers) owned black African slaves. Things have since been added but nothing has been revised or changed to include all people that now occupy this place we refer to as a melting pot or mosaic.

A black man's fate is just as worse when he is released from the captivity of his prison cell. He cannot register to vote; this means he has no political voice or input to help shape and inspire the selection of worthy politicians or voting for the passage of certain bills. Many employers are reluctant to hire newly released convicts. Difficulty seeking legitimate employment is one of the main reasons why many black males end up right back in prison; they are forced to resort back to their criminal tactics for economic gain. Of course, the system is rigged this way. White males previously incarcerated do not face as nearly the same job difficulties. White privilege and white supremacy are accountable for a white ex-convicts ability to bounce right back from adversity.

Many blacks living in Baltimore's inner-city experience a hard time finding employment within their community, period. They are surrounded by liquor stores, laundromats, grocers, local restaurants, and other places of business that are not black owned, and these businesses have no desire to hire blacks; although, they are not the least bit reluctant to take black money and revenue. It is a humiliating and degrading experience for one to be purposefully cut out of the opportunity to legitimately make money within their own community. I found it peculiar to hear so many of the outsiders (non-residents of Baltimore) cry out that those involved in the riots were tearing down their own communities, because these people have no idea that most places that they were looting were not black owned, and many were commercialized businesses with plenty insurance to cover the claims of property damage and theft. Those on the outside looking in were just playing into the trap that news and media had set up all along. They wanted to mesh Baltimore's riot situation into the collage of other black male vs. police/legal system situations. Not to digress, Baltimore Riots of 2015 will be discussed in a latter chapter.

The incarceration of black males mean sons absent from their family, fathers' estranged from children, educational/employment opportunities deferred or lost. Prison destroys dreams and hopes. Redemption is possible; but it is much harder for the black male as it is in comparison to his white counterpart. Even if he is remorseful, has learned from his crime, and constructively served his time, he is still welcomed with folded arms and wrinkled brows. This maltreatment and unforgiving approach will teach a black male that he is not even allowed to make a mistake in American's society. Under the auspices of white supremacy, the black male is already perceived as a threat and a genetic flaw. He is ill-equipped to fight an infrastructure that has been conditioned to oppress, suppress, and force subservience upon him and his ancestors. His vices are dull in a society that provides no history on him and his black people before the institution of slavery. If he is a young black male, he is not too familiar with slavery at all. He only knows the minimum that we have all learned through western education. He has nothing to go by to feel significant. If he lives in the inner-city, he will surely have his firsthand experience with law enforcement, whether he is abiding by the law or not. Those law enforcement agents that bully him within his community will not all be white. As a matter of fact, in Baltimore City, the police officers are predominantly black. Therefore, white supremacy employees other minorities to keep the others in check. While there are officers black and white who will see the problem of the system and how Baltimore City is set up, there are countless others who will partake in the system and its legal corruption with pride.

How Black Children are Impacted by Black Male Incarceration

As I mentioned, it is a losing situation for families of the black incarcerated male. If he has progeny, they may rebel out of loss of their father. This rebellious behavior can manifest in the household, school, or other social settings. Consequently, those children who give into the rebellion are more susceptible to fall into the tempting and dangerous lures of the inner-city streets. Another individual may replace the role of the father, and prepare that child for the same fate as his actual father.

The streets are a cold and desolate place for youth. Most of the lessons are barbaric in nature and primal instinct rules the day. We live in such a Darwinist society, where this conditioning is welcomed, and the governing officials overlook the misfortunes impoverished community. Our children must beware of the odds that are purposefully placed against them. They have a better chance at this when black males combine with others to stand as a pillars in the community. We have too many drug dealers, drug addicts, drop-outs, and deadbeats. There are many black males defying the stereotype and jail hype. However, it is not so many of them to have a significant impact in the inner-city, when many are locked up behind bars.

Naturally, the first example a kid has of a man comes from the male parent. Many male children emulate the behaviors of their fathers, and aspire to be like their father. Black fathers have no place in prison. Black males have no place in there as a whole. However, the black father's condition often begets that of the black son. This a most contributing factor to black males being in prison. Following the role of the father. Therefore, black males must beware that they are not teaching the children to emulate a pattern of destruction and failure.

CHAPTER 6

DETERMINING INTERVENTION METHODS FOR BALTIMORE'S BLACK YOUTH

I almost wanted to go into the in depth of empirical and peer-reviewed research methods. However, I have covered that in chapter 3 and chapter 4 of this book. What is truly needed in this particular chapter is an approach from those black inner-city members, who have firsthand knowledge of what goes on in their own communities and what is needed. Being a current graduate scholar, and potential licensed counselor practitioner, I have received the various coursework and practicum/internship preparation, and training for the field of counseling psychology. Of all the clinical studies I have reviewed about prevention intervention, majority of them are by non-black clinicians and researchers. Most or nearly all of which are white. One may ask what the problem with this is. They are professionals, right? They received the scholarly preparation and training to universally understand the cognitive, physiological, emotional, and social conditions of all beings regardless of race, right? The truth of the matter is that European psychologists, European philosophers, and European theorists developed ideologies specifically for maintaining the order and system of white supremacy. Therefore, their limited and poorly conducted studies on blacks have been systematically designed to be such a way since the inception of modern day westernized psychology. I have grown to understand that intelligence testing in school has little to do with monitoring the capabilities and aptitude of the child. As it pertains to schooling in the black community, intelligence testing aka aptitude school tests are all about making sure the progress of the black child is to an academic minimum. Therefore, it should come as no surprise that many black inner-city schools go on unchecked by the city of Baltimore's Board of Education. Most times schools are audited or sort out when there is gentrification (white financially affluent population/integration of whites into poor and black neighborhoods). The Board of Education knows that white affluent homeowners or renters are going to want to know where the best schools are within their vicinity. They demand a community with the best and healthiest grocers and markets. They want parks for dog walking and places to dispense the waste of their dogs. As a proud dog owner, I, myself, cannot get a park that allows for me to walk my dog, and I live around the corner from two well-known parks in west Baltimore's uptown inner-city. However, if I go into the downtown area near Baltimore's Harbor, Federal Hill, Fells Point, or Canton area, I can find all of the parks with doggy bags and doggy water dispensers, and waste baskets. There is definitely an intended and purposeful demarcated boundary. A modern day version of Charles Dickens tale of two cities within the same city. Government owned housing properties in Baltimore's inner-city have literally collapsed and fallen on young children and adults (two of these building collapses where reported as fatal; one recently occurred earlier 2016 involving an elderly black man). The local and state government are blatantly conveying to black inner-city members through negligence, how much it really gives a care about our black neighborhoods and blacks in general. Kind of hard and shocking to believe, considering the fact that Baltimore currently has a black woman as mayor, a black woman District Attorney, and several local officials and council members that are majority black as well. Could it be that every one of our council members (including the black council leaders of Baltimore) are in on the socio-economical degradation, psychological deterioration, and ethnic annihilation Baltimore black citizens? It is no longer a coincidence, when every inner-city street where there are majority blacks is cratered; all of the buildings are dilapidated, caving in and collapsing on people, all of the drug treatment (particularly heroin/meth centers) are strategically placed in the inner-city community; inferior public schooling is broad throughout every Baltimore City district; liquor stores are present on just about every street corner, and drugs of all sorts are available on a smorgasbord of the black inner-city streets. This is far from a coincidence; but, nothing shy of a dead-on orchestrated trap. Therefore, we have to take all of these things into consideration when asking ourselves what an intervention for black youth in Baltimore would consist of. Biasedly, the white supremacist infrastructure that allows for these conditions, would opt to have all of our black children evaluated and medicated for life. It has been proven that doping our children makes them more susceptible to be institutionalized within a correctional facility or problems with drug abuse, and the law. This is the white supremacist method of intervention for our black children.

What is needed to Help Our Youth?

I cannot emphasize enough, the importance of healthy black households. The abundant existence of healthy black inner-city households is insufficient. One main reason behind this is both redundant and thoroughly reiterated because it is the main ingredient: perpetuated impoverished conditions brought on by white supremacist strategies to oppress and suppress the black race. In other words, ghettoization has been a most effective tool in destroying many ethnic groups. Hitler exercised this with the Jews during the Holocaust era. European powers have exercised this with South Africa during the Apartheid era, and so forth, have they in other parts of Africa and the world abroad. In order to get to the root of the needs for the youth, one must aim to discover and cure the needs of the caretakers of our youth that have been victimized by a system designed and responsible for their condition of impoverishment. A healthy household anywhere cannot exist if the parties of that household are unaware and blind to the roots of their own oppression. Information on the subject matter is powerful, and the caretakers of our inner-city can become empowered once given the knowledge and tools necessary to maneuver within a social system that promotes subjugation, self-abnegation, and racial stratification.

The constant familiarization with the social climatic conditioning that has been put into play, needs to be taught by black community members that are capable and express the desire to be leaders. No longer can the self-proclaimed enlightened ones of our community hide their capabilities and power to transform, and uplift the others of the community who are unaware of how to influence their youth and empower themselves. Many of us watch the lost ones of our community with abhorrent disgust. Although we understand the system, we watch the misguided of our community wander aimlessly. A few of us will help, and others will carry on with our lives; absent of compassion and ignorant to the powerful sentiment of sympathy. In a strong sense, those of us who operate like this, have subconsciously taken on the mindset of the white supremacist. Those individuals' ideologies have been transformed from that of black pride to bitter disdain and self-loathing. These individuals ultimately begin to believe that they are separate from other blacks, and that there is no real "negro problem" as DuBois mentioned in his *Souls of Black Folk*. The black enlightened community must beware of embracing white supremacist ideologies because they will become pawns in the system to destroy their own people. Truth be told, we have black politicians, black pastors, black teachers, so-called black activists, and other types of black leaders who are agents advocating white supremacy. Those of us who intend to sincerely lead our community must protect our black children from the follies and ideologies of these black false prophets.

Community Fostering

Community fostering is necessity in our communities. The inner-city is allowed to remain in its present condition, because we do not organize and develop inclusively within our black communities. We complain about what is going on and may protest a most highlighted community tragedy (i.e. Baltimore Riots/Freddie Gray). However, we do not readily challenge the officials we elect to lead or communities. Nor do we combine our financial resources to create our own banks, stores, schools, community centers, and other resources for our communities to thrive. Majority of the resources within our community are owned by outsiders and non-blacks (mainly Asians and Arabs). We do not encourage and promote ourselves to be our own business owners and distributors. The Asians and Arabs have their own private and/or inclusive communities that cater to their race and culture. We need to do the same as black folk. State, local, and federal funded subsidies will only go so far in the black inner-city community. Besides, the funding is allocated and regulated specifically for keeping blacks limited socially and economically. Those of us who have acquired wealth or an abundant source of income are eligible to network amongst ourselves to establish our own financial funding centers. In Baltimore City, there are tons of dilapidated and rehab dwellings that can now be purchased for little to nothing. Improving these dwellings to make them habitable for other blacks, whether they are low-income or totally impoverished, can improve the quality of life and self-esteem of those persons alone. Adequate and dignified housing fosters a strong sense of community.

When our children have sufficient and quality housing, they have a safe haven from poverty, and squalor no longer appears as a normative condition. Social service funding is not meant to prevent nor eliminate the ghettoization within the black inner-city. It is deliberately scanty apportioned to maintain such a condition and state. Social, economic, and political disparity exists in white supremacist America to keep the black and poor disenfranchised on every level. This is why organizing and accounting for our own earnings in order to build our community is essential, and a must. Many foreigners come to America to work and save money to help their relatives and race. We cannot depend on the government that has long disadvantaged us to uplift us from our social status. The "power of the purse" gives one power to utilize his or her funds as they see fit. Power of the purse gives our children the opportunity to attend college or university, afford housing, and receive employment opportunities. The creation of our own financial institutes will provide for community needs without our children having to outsource their skills in a corporate environment that has no real concern for their advancement or well-being.

Schooling for Us and By Us

Renowned black psychologist, Umar Johnson, had a great vision for a school that would benefit our black male youth. However, for whatever reason, his vision did not take flight. Perhaps his vision can serve as a precursor for all blacks to start considering schooling for our black youth. We can no longer expect the government to make any real progress on improving inferior schooling in the black community. We also cannot equate inferior education to the availability of finance that allot students to have the latest textbooks and educational technology. Adequate schooling for our children extends beyond the availability of money and technology. In fact, there were black schools that were more successful, and influential during the times of Jim Crow. This is because black community leaders served as educators and taught black youth the history of who they are as a people. That was very necessary under a racially charged climate that has done (and continues to do) all that it could to prevent blacks from learning. The latter is still important this present day and time. We must create academic settings that are ran and operated by black educators. The curricula must deviate from the westernized educational system that teaches false truths. Our children must understand the history or their origins. Black history in education is not limited to the history of enslavement, but also teaching our children the role that their ancestors played in various subjects such as; math, art, science, literature, and other traditional subjects.

When our children are in a learning environment that excludes them, they can easily become discouraged and frustrated with such an academic system. The media and its statistics would like to convince us that our children our incapable of learning, and staying focused. How can a race of children focus in a system that has absolutely no suggestions or solutions to elevate them from their current condition? It is truly impossible for a black child to identify with himself/herself in a schooling system that aims to intentionally brainwash them with Eurocentric theories and teachings. They need a black Afrocentric point-of-view which educates them and enlightens them about their ethnicity and heritage. Collectively, our culture is capitalized off of and bastardized within America. We have been hijacked for our soul, our coolness, and vibrant spirits. After being drained of such, we have been made to drain and destroy ourselves under the auspices of white supremacy. The cycle will continue for our black youth if we fail to clip and detach them America's toxic umbilical cord that is pumping self-hate into the immune system of our children.

Implications on Intervention for Black Youth

Intervention does not start with the saturated and limited psychological case studies researchers conduct on our black youth. It starts with the black leaders and elders of today. We must reinvent the African tradition of factual lore of our history's past and present. As events of our existence of a people are unfolding, we should be taking notes, and documenting our progress as a people. We cannot depend on television to teach our children the true history of themselves. We cannot allow technology to desensitize and distract our children from making progress is today's society. Most of our black youth assume that the American dream is living as well-to-do white people. They must understand that America was built off of the labor and blood of our African ancestors. If our youth do not understand where they fit into the equation of America, they will fall for almost every lie fed to them by the white supremacist ideologists that run the world. They will believe that there is absolutely no hope for our race. They will actually believe that we are inferior and ignorant beings. We must divulge of the facts and information of who we are to promote self-love amongst our black youth.

Youth centers that promote life-enhancing skills, workshops, recreation, and celebration are much needed in Baltimore's inner-city. Upon her induction into the mayor's office, Stephanie Rawlings-Blake closed several recreational centers. These centers gave our inner-city youth something exciting to look forward to. They were free and very accommodating to black inner-city parents who cannot afford camp or childcares services. These community centers often offered events to engage both parent and child into activities that increase family time and bonding. Truly, one would think a mayor would not destroy a system and a foundation that actually works. Most of those that offer activities in the community centers do it voluntarily. Clearly, Mrs. Rawlings-Blake's intention were for the best interests of those who are not within Baltimore city's black communities. This does not necessarily mean it was for whites either. Mrs. Rawlings-Blake is a prime example of a corrupt politician. Her first few years in office, she took her family and friends to celebrate the Baltimore Raven's super bowl in New Orleans's French Quarter district. This was alleged to be funded by Baltimoreans taxpaying wages. This is just a snippet of her mismanaging of government money. The money spent could have been used to fund the recreational centers she closed; it was taxpayers' money anyway, and should have been used to improve our community. As mentioned, we cannot depend on the government to benefit our youth. We have to organize our own centers through our community churches, black business owners, and other black community members who have access to venue that can be used for the purposes of engaging our youth in recreational events. Community organized centers can be a headquarters for mentoring, educating, and training our youth. It can be utilized for more than fun and sport and keeping youth off the street. It can be used to help youth acquire jobs, scholarships, diplomas, and other vocational related services.

Solidarity and community commitment is a great way to promote intervention. Mothers, fathers, aunts, uncles and so forth need to maintain a vigilant and active role within the community. They need to interact amongst one another to demonstrate the influence of unity through positive and affective communication. Kids of all colors learn by example. If they witness ongoing dysfunction between members of their community and family, they will participate in such dysfunction because it normalized within their environment. Therefore, we must show our black youth that more problems get solved by talking to find solutions versus warring or fighting. A team is very effective when every player uses his or her position to advance the team as a whole versus individually. Altruistic behavior will also teach our youth that helping others also will also benefit them on a personal level.

Chapter 7

GOVERNMENT NEGLIGENCE AND SOCIAL CORRUPTION

Baltimore City is not known for the most prominent city council members. In fact, quite a few Baltimore City government officials (including the former mayor of Baltimore, Sharon Dixon) have been caught in fraudulent activities and scandals. Over the years, there have been numerous cops from Baltimore City and Baltimore County, engaging in drug smuggling and trafficking. There have been Baltimore officers, who have shot at one another in clubs. A few years ago, a Baltimore City officer barricaded himself and his wife in their home and killed her, and he then committed suicide. There is even a Huffington Post (2013) interview of former Baltimore police sergeant Michael A. Wood, Jr. describing in detail a plethora of corruption by the Baltimore police officers. All of which have been swept under the rug. He describes in detail the horrific things Baltimore's police have done to the citizens of Baltimore. Their dirty deeds have all gone unpunished and unchecked. How can we expect to have justice in the inner-city when the ones tasked with upholding and enforcing the law are the ones committing more offenses than the individuals they are both legally and unlawfully accosting? It is obvious that this activity would be need not apply when our city council members can clearly, visually, and physically see the epidemic of community negligence taking place in black communities. Meanwhile, our children our deemed to see this type of living as normal and typical of a black community. They automatically assume that the condition of the people are solely from the people who inhabit that community. This perception has the potential for arousing self-abnegation, self-loathing, and demoralizing behaviors and conduct. If you do not see yourself as a significant factor within your community, it becomes hard to see any change or impact you can bring to that community.

I developed specific survey questions that asked questions surrounding around redlining, gentrification, and its impact on people of color. A very good confident of mines who has worked to improve the quality Baltimore's Housing projects and programs acquired firsthand knowledge from professional experience, and community involvement. Even through her own personal pursuits, and endeavors, she is still dedicated and interested in the quality living of those of low socioeconomic status. Below is her responses to the problems that exist in the community as it pertains to housing and socioeconomic conditioning of the inner-city community.

Survey

1. Please explain redlining?

Lykinda

Historically, redlining was a tactic that was used to keep mortgagers and other housing investors from investing in undesirable neighborhoods. These neighborhoods would be described as neighborhoods that were not homogenous and neighborhoods that were made up of blacks and Mexicans. Maps were drawn and neighborhoods were separated by colors. The neighborhoods outlined in red were the "redlined" or bad neighborhoods that denied mortgages and other investments simply because of the racial makeup. Redlining has evolved over the years as the Federal Housing Agency has declared redlining in its original form as illegal. New forms of redlining include subprime lending, devaluing of homes in poor and less desirable neighborhoods, and the shutting out of qualified black and other minority buyers out of certain "upscale" neighborhoods.

2. What significant impact does redlining have on poor neighborhoods?

Redlining is one of the most significant forms of systematic racism instituted by the Government. It keeps the poor, especially blacks, poor. If your grandparents were denied a loan in the 30s through the 50s for a home that they qualified for simply because they were black, then the chances are that their descendants are still struggling in poverty. Your home is the biggest part of your wealth. It is the biggest part of wealth that is passed through families.

3. Why is redlining utilized?

Lykinda

Redlining is used to oppress people of color as well as low-income people. Redlining is also used to keep the values of homes in more desirable neighborhoods from losing value by shutting out the less desirable populations that can afford to and may wish to live there. For instance, many black professionals making upwards of $100K per year are living next to and in neighborhoods with white neighbors making less than half of what they do.

Denise Morris

1. How does gentrification affect the poor in Baltimore
    City?

    Lykinda
    Gentrification disrupts the daily lives and culture of the
    black and poor in Baltimore City by displacing people
    from their homes. Gentrification also furthers the
    damaging perception that the only way to have a good
    neighborhood and services is by having an affluent white
    neighborhood.

2. What does gentrification mean for Baltimore City
    adolescents?

    Lykinda
    Gentrification lowers the moral for adolescents and the
    youth that are displaced from their homes. People are
    being "priced out" of homes they have spent their entire
    lives in. They are no longer welcome in neighborhoods
    that they once thrived in. For the youth, they become
    even more hopeless and their self-worth is highly
    affected because they feel like their opinions, lives, and
    homes do not matter to those in positions of power.

3. How and when does gentrification occur? What can we do in the black community to combat against gentrification?

Lykinda

Gentrification occurs when a major redevelopment of a lower income community occurs and the current residents are priced out or can no longer afford to live in their neighborhoods. They are relocated or forced to find different housing accommodations because the entire structure of their neighborhood has been changed by the "gentry's" moving in. For instance, in major cities around the country, the current trend is that inner cities are being taken over by "gentry's" through gentrification and the usual urban dwellers are being forced to move to more suburban areas. In Baltimore in particular, all high rise public housing developments were leveled and new communities were built using the mixed-finance/income model through federal Hope VI grants. The new communities did not allow for a one-for-one replacement of families that were displaced after the projects were demolished. The new communities are a mix of all income levels and all housing types. There are market rate rentals, homeownership, affordable rental, and affordable homeownership all in one development.

Gentrification occurs for several different reasons. Most of them are political and are cited as public safety concerns. The desirability of certain areas is also a huge reason for gentrification. For instance, in Baltimore, after the Casino was built in close proximity to both stadiums in the South Baltimore/Pig Town area, development in that area sky rocketed as well as housing values and desirability. The name of the neighborhood was renamed Washington Village, the Main Street businesses are 95% occupied and running, and this neighborhood is now a desired location for middle and upper middle class citizens. The fabric of the neighborhood as well as the faces of those in the neighborhood are rapidly changing.

Since gentrification cannot happen without political approval or motivation, the best way for neighborhoods to combat this is to be involved in their community organizations. Stay apprised of any proposed developments, attend meetings concerning those developments, and quite frankly become NIMBY'S. NIMBY'S are the not in my back yard neighbors that oppose basically anything that changes their neighborhoods as they know it. Baltimore City lists all neighborhood associations and the phone numbers on

the Baltimore City website: www.baltimorecity.gov. Be
active in your communities! GET INVOLVED!

1. Explain differences in quality and equality between
    affluent Baltimore City neighborhoods and
    impoverished Baltimore City neighborhoods.

Lykinda

The main contrast between neighborhoods of the
affluent and poor in Baltimore City is the availability of
quality goods and services. In most cases, even if those
goods and services are available in the poorer or less
desirable parts of town, they are more expensive than in
affluent areas. For instance, available city, state, and
some federal funds are allocated to states and
municipalities comparable to the tax base of those areas.
If you have areas that have little to no homeownership,
therefore no taxes, then the schools in those areas are
labeled "bad". They are bad because of the perceived
quality of the student that attends, the achievements of
the students that attend, and also the quality of the
teachers that teach there. Another stark difference
between affluent and poor neighborhoods is the access to
quality and affordable food. Most poor neighborhoods
in Baltimore City qualify as food deserts. A food desert
is by definition an urban area where it is difficult to buy

good-quality and affordable fresh food. The lack of
fresh food leads to poor health in many and poor health
is also a direct effect of poverty and is correlated to
where you live.

2. Explain the benefits and disadvantages between the two
   neighborhoods.

Lykinda

The major advantages that affluent neighborhoods have
over poor disadvantaged neighborhoods is quality
healthcare, the availability of quality fresh food, good
schools, political clout, and almost everything is
cheaper. The next time you are riding around in your
city, take a look at simple things like gas prices,
convenience store prices, how many grocery stores there
are, and how clean or trashy neighborhoods are.
Baltimore City offers a cleaning service to
neighborhoods that are willing to pay extra taxes to keep
their neighborhood's clean. Since we know that poor
people do not own their homes in the city for the most
part or most are struggling, this is a service that is of
little to no benefit to them. Not only is the availability
of goods and services a stark difference, but the types of
goods and services offered in the different
neighborhoods is different. There are liquor stores, vape

stores, high-priced convenience stores, and pizza and sub shops on every corner in low-income areas. In areas of affluence, you have strip malls with restaurants, grocery stores, nail salons, barber shops, neighborhood green spaces, and many pockets of parks and recreations scattered throughout the areas. It's literally like living in two totally different worlds. The biggest difference is the culture that children are being taught and the experiences in their everyday lives.

3. Does class and race play a factor when it comes to the conditions of these neighborhoods?

Lykinda

Class and race has everything to do with the conditions of these neighborhoods. In particular the redlining that stems from the 1930's that was a government mandate on banks receiving federal funds is the specific root of the problem. The systemic racism through the denial of equal equity, safety, education, housing, and the American dream has led to the continued downfall of the poor and black in the United States.

Denise Morris

VERIFICATION

Please include the following for referencing purposes:

1. Please include your job or Duty titles and the role you play(ed) in the Baltimore City housing development.

Lykinda

Former Controller of the Planning and Development Department of the Housing Authority of Baltimore City 10 years. Former Chief Financial Manager of D.C. Housing Enterprises, a subsidiary of the D.C. Housing Authority, Current CFO of Baltimore Now, a real estate development consulting firm. Current CFO of 28 Walker Associates, a real estate Development Firm.

2. Please include your years of experience.

Lykinda

20 years of affordable housing and real estate development experience at the local and federal level. 5 years of experience in commercial real estate development and property management. A certified Housing Development Finance Professional, Certified New Markets Tax Credits professional, Certified Management Accountant, a passionate activist for equality for poor and disenfranchised people.

3. Please include how you would like to be named or referenced in my book.

Lykinda

A passionate activist for equality for poor and disenfranchised people. This is the proudest of all of my titles. My name is Lykinda Camper.

Implications Based Upon the Survey

Lykinda Camper's detailed analysis stems from professional experience, and activism within the communities that constantly face the issues of gentrification and redlining. She explained what redlining is and it is definitely a practice to disenfranchise blacks and other minorities (namely Hispanics or Latinos). This demarcating line have been established around the times of Jim Crow, the Great Depression era, and they exist in modern form (subprime lending, and devaluing property, as Lykinda Camper mentioned in the survey). The online website Investopedia (2016) describes subprime as "high risk" mortgages often offered to individuals with a credit score under 600. Subprime lenders use poor credit scores against these individuals, and jack up the mortgage interest rates for the loan. The sad thing is that these lenders are like loan sharks and can hike up the interest rates to such an exorbitant amount that the payee has choice but to forfeit the loan. This type of negligent investor behavior often forces people to lose housing, declare bankruptcy, consolidation, and liquidation of their financial funds and assets. It is such a cruel game played intentionally to deprave individuals of color and the poor from gaining a chance to establish and build credit. Furthermore, this is the modern legal covert act of redlining. Just as prison for minorities, and blacks is slavery by another name. Subprime lending can cause permanent damage or long-term damage to one's financial health and credit. This is how individuals (particularly blacks and poor) die owing or trying to pay off outrageous mortgage loans with tons of interest.

My question as researcher is how one combat modern day redlining that is legally categorized as something else? One way to combat against redlining is to recognize the behavior and legislatures that makes it illegal or unlawful to practice redlining. The Fair Housing Act (FHAct), under title VIII of the Civil Rights Act of 1968, declares it "unlawful" to discriminate upon individuals on the basis of ethnicity, disability, religion, familial background, and gender. *Lowballing* is considered another form of redlining. According the Fair Housing Act (FHAct), under title VIII of the Civil Rights Act of 1968, lowballing is defined as "the practice of making an excessively low appraisal in relation to the purchase price on the basis of prohibited considerations." This is when the appraising party markets the value of the property for lower than it is actually worth. This causes potential buyers to opt out of purchasing the property because the loan is more than the property amount (FHAct). In addition, the FHAct code of regulations described the use of racial images to draw a particular ethnic group, deliberately making insurance unavailable, and the use of unnecessary elaborate qualification processes as other forms of housing discrimination. Understanding these amendments and other policies that ensure equality along the basis of homeownership, loans, grants, or any other socioeconomically related vices equips blacks with the knowledge and ability to distinguish between discrimination and fair treatment. Many of us often become misled because we bypass reading the fine print when we venture to make life changing decisions. One cannot afford to take such risk when it comes to property and ownership.

Gentrification

When many hear the term gentrification, they envision conglomerate businesses and realtor companies bulldozing through historically and predominantly black or minority areas to construct unaffordable housing, and open up multiple savvy businesses that causes the cost of mortgage to go up for the residents of the smaller businesses as well as the property value for the inhabitants. All of this is true in the sense of how gentrification plays out into the inner-city. Lykinda, gave a very great example, when she mentioned the gentrification of south Baltimore due to the erection of the new Horseshoe Casino. Stated that the property value went up because of this; meaning the cost of living has become more expensive for the inhabitants of south Baltimore.

Denise Morris

Combating gentrification may be very difficult. As Lykinda mentioned, gentrification is political. This means our local officials (mayors, governors, city councilmen) may make decisions with outsiders in order to boost the economic morale of Baltimore as a whole but they fail to see how this hurts the people. Meanwhile, many who engage in these practices are very much aware of the effects of allowing businesses to come into poorer or black neighborhoods and take over. Mayor Rawlings-Blake and the others lied to the citizens of Baltimore City big time. The main reason, the Baltimore city council emphasized the need for the casino, was to utilize the money accrued from the casino to fund the public schools in order to improve the quality, and schooling conditions for our youth. Yet, and still, our schools are ill-equipped, many dilapidated with no heat or air, limited textbooks, and lagging or unabundant technology. In defense against allowing this again, we must exercise our right to vote to elect individuals that have a history of serving the needs of the community with integrity, passion, and concern. We must closely examine the track records of those we allow to govern our lives. They are many crooked politicians sitting in council seats in every city; however, we must be concerned with those who fit that description in Baltimore City. There are some members who have overextended their stay. We must invest in our communities. This means supporting affluent businesses that have been in our community for a long period of time. If we help them stay in business, we may not have to worry about competitive businesses coming in from the outside to overthrow our local businesses.

Very soon, Catherine Pugh, the newly elected mayor of Baltimore City, will be in office. Considering her campaign strategy, one can say she leaves much to be desired. For instance, she lured blacks in the urban community or inner-city into voting by placing them on party buses, with the offer of a few dollars and a "chicken box" (otherwise known in Baltimore as carryout fried wings, with fries, a biscuit, and a can soda). Other people (black poor residents of Baltimore City) have told me that Pugh had her campaign employees tell them that they were giving out jobs and to come to a selected center in the city (which was actually facility set up with voting booths) to fill out an application for employment. This is the most exploitive campaign strategy I have ever heard of in my life. This is especially of low moral character for an elected official that is supposed to demonstrate the upmost support, and compassion for the people she services within the community. Another sad fact, is Pugh is an African American woman. The act that she pulled makes her a political anomaly to the black people she serves, and her own cultural identity. How can a woman who claims to know the needs of the community exploit individuals who are ignorant and unaware of her exploits? It is obvious to those of us who are aware that she opted buy the people's vote. Unfortunately, she succeeded. It is even sadder that our council members did not challenge her method of campaigning. This is slavish bribery.

111

They impeached the former mayor (Sheila Dixon, who actually ran up against Catherine Pugh) for taking bribes when she was in office. Nothing is being said about a woman who hasn't even taken her seat in the mayor's office as she comes giving bribes. Elected mayor Pugh may be the one to accept bribes from major corporations that favor to turn Baltimore City into a smorgasbord for the financially affluent whites.

As Lykinda mentioned in the survey interview, the individuals within the community need to become involved in organizations within the community that combat against gentrification and political corruption. Lykinda proposed the idea of becoming a NIMBY (not in my backyard neighbor), an individual who is against big time developers coming into to their communities and revamping the structure and culture of their neighborhood. We must take it upon ourselves to acquaint with our city councilmen and discuss any up and coming housing or community projects that may be detrimental to our longevity in our community.

CHAPTER 8

ADDRESSING NEGLIGENCE AND ABUSE OF BLACK YOUTH

Many blacks that have experienced or endured abuse have done so since youth at the expense of biological parents, legal guardians, or caretakers. Sexual abuse is thematic in many black households. It is often kept secret amongst relatives. Such incidents have even occurred in my family and relatives have swept it under the rug. Usually, the male is the perpetrator and the female relatives (mother, sisters, and aunts) partake in keeping it a secret. It is not surprising to hear them deflect the allegation and blame it on you by being too fast (a saying that black women often tell the pubescent black female relatives, because she is perceived as too physically developed or mature for her age; all of which she has no physical control over). I refer to this type of blaming as the *'you brought it on yourself syndrome'*. The women that aim to protect the perpetrator shames the adolescent child that has been sexually abused. The child (often the black female adolescent) is told that is it all her fault. It is unclear to me whether black women participating in this shaming do so to protect the black male because of the harshness of the judicial system toward black men as far as penalties and crime are concerned. Maybe the fear of losing their

113

sons, husbands, fathers, nephews, or brothers to the penal system altogether compels them to take an oath of secrecy. Regardless of their reason or choice, these actions can have long lasting effects upon the adolescent victims. Child abuse can ultimately alter a child's self-esteem and that will alter their behavioral patterns, and possibly lead to psychological or mental disorders. Adults in our community, whether male or female, need to be aware of how they are just as guilty as the perpetrator of the abuse when they refuse to come forth. They also need to be aware that they are prolonging the endangerment of the adolescent when they do not reveal this information to the necessary parties.

Children that are abused are more susceptible to risqué behavior such as drug use, alcohol abuse, unprotected sex, teenage pregnancy, and other comparative behaviors. Their cries must not be neglected, and any form of abuse must be taken seriously and looked into in order to secure the safety of our black children. As an inspiring and potential counseling psychology professional that has previously and currently studied under licensed counseling professionals and social workers, it is not uncommon for them to reveal to me that many of the abuse amongst black inner-city adolescents is either physical or sexual in nature. Furthermore, deeper research and therapy sessions have revealed that it is most likely that the adolescents' parent was a victim of physical or sexual abuse some point and time in their adolescent stages. This may be one explanation for the shaming. Perhaps the parent tried to be vocal and tell someone he/she trusted in confidence, only to be dissuaded in saying anything further on the matter, through shaming, and being made to feel as if they were responsible for the abuse rendered unto them as a child. Consequently, behavior perpetuates, and is generationally passed along if it remains unchecked. Therefore, the abused adult must be consoled and counseled in order to understand the importance in exposing this wickedly sick practice. If not, they subject their child to the same ills. Especially, if the abuser is an active or present figure in that child's life. Allowing an adolescent to be subjected to physical abuse and/or sexual abuse sends a powerfully disturbing message that fractures their self-esteem, and clouds a healthy image of one's self. It also sends a message to our children that their body does not matter, and can be violated at any time without retribution or punishment.

There are too many media images and day-to-day occurrences that shows our black race being killed and wrongfully murdered by law enforcement agents, and amongst ourselves. This sends another negative message to our children that their bodies, and minds are underappreciated and disregarded under a white supremacist system. As youths, such a system conditions our black children to accept the brutalities rendered under them. However, if we are also participating in this brutalization (directly or indirectly) we ourselves, are then guilty of upholding a system by engaging in the destruction of

115

ourselves and our black youth as well. Now is the time to restore the self-image of our black people, and our black children by crushing and debunking those negative stereotypes that categorize our existence as worthless. Our youth will one day be the future leaders of tomorrow. Our children must understand that every intricate part of their existence is just as worthy as any other child or human being upon this universe.

Negligence and abuse of children is a serious matter in the United States and countries abroad. The U.S. Department of Health and Human Services (DHS, 2014) and National Children's Alliance (NCA, 2015) Statistical Fact Sheet reveals that nearly 80% of fatal child abuse cases are caused by one or both of the adolescents parents. Furthermore, infant children were more susceptible to higher rates of child abuse than other age groups of kids in the United States. This further confirms the fact that most child abuse occurrences happen in the household by the parent or close relative.

CHAPTER 9

HOW DOES WHITE SUPRECMACY EFFECT US ALL?

This is a very sensitive subject, especially to those who are a part of this system that are not willing to deal with the issue of white supremacy. It is the proverbial elephant in the room that divides those who float on the demographics between race, class, and social status. Systematically and intentionally, white supremacy is meant to benefit "supreme whites". Who are supreme whites? One must explore the origins of white supremacy before such a question can be answered. Many historians argue that the spark of white supremacy (although not referred under the title *white supremacy*) began with King Ferdinand and Queen Isabella of Spain. Their funding of Spanish navigator and conquest, Christopher Columbus, is what led to slavery in North America (i.e. enslavement of African slaves via Atlantic Slave Trade). European colonizers also bribed, conquered, and killed natives of America in order to gain territory and power over the land; hence, power over what we know as the United States of America today. Another argument is that European empires (Greece and Rome) of the earliest centuries built their legacy through conquering and enslaving other Europeans. This entails European monarchies overthrowing one another and forcing the conquered parties and their kingdom into servitude or harsh slavery. Many white supremacists' extremist groups honor and pay homage to Hitler for influencing the Aryan nation and Nazism, where he stressed that blond hair and blue eyed Europeans where the truest, and superior above any race; further, his antisemitism, lead to a brutal event for Jews known as the Holocaust. In 2016, the Ku Klux Klan (KKK) and other white supremacist groups are overtly resurfacing due to the hatred spread from Trumps presidential nomination and campaigning. These are all forms of white supremacy from a historical timeframe, from past to present.

The underlying theme of white supremacy is just that "white supreme groups". This is by class and also by race of Europeans. For instance, Hitler declared that white blue-eyed and blond hair Germans were the true superior Europeans. Many monarch families of Europe declared that they were meant to rule over all Europeans on the continent of Europe. With this being said, white supremacy can either include or exclude its own on the basis or ethnic origins and class. This is one way that all ethnic groups (including other whites) and races in America are affected by white supremacy. It is a historical and statistical fact that African Americans in America are most affected by white supremacy. Many uncivil injustices have been practiced toward us by white supremacist since our inception in America. Regardless of numbers, we must all understand as Americans, the harm of participating in the system of white supremacy, whether as victim or victimizer. It is also helpful to know that white supremacist use pawns to carry out their orders in order to eternally perpetuate the tyrannical system of white supremacy.

The Key Players in the White Supremacist System

Oppressors/Dictators

The white supremacist are the oppressors and dictators. This means that they have social, economic, and military/political control. Those four variables are the elements of their power and how they are able to stay in control. Majority our American institutions, organizations, and corporations are funded, ran, and established by white supremacists. White supremacist in this tone means white elite individuals, parties, or families that own majority of the wealth. Therefore, they own majority of the property and land. These beings are the puppeteers who pull all the strings, and can either make or break you with one crucial move. They rule our government, judicial/legal system, banking/financial institutions, and enforce social order that revolves around one's subordination to their power. The Constitution was drafted and developed by the "Forefathers" and fashioned and tailor-made for individuals in the same ruling class as themselves; other elitist descendants.

Employees/Enforcers

White supremacists hire individuals to do their bidding. They are the agents that enforce the executive orders that have been given in order to protect and maintain the power of their elite masters. These individuals are usually in high ranks within corporations, businesses or organizations. They are the CEO's, presidents', top ranking military personnel, and the likes. They exercise power and influence on a macrocosmic level; meaning their power trickles down from the top of the chain to the bottom of the chain in terms of authority. It is not uncommon to see high ranking officials (e.g. current President Obama) ridiculed, belittled, humiliated, and disgraced for stepping outside of the boundaries of white supremacy. It is important to understand that the agent also has agents to enforce order if they step out of line. The bureaucratic checks-and-balance system ensures that there is also an all watching eye watching the other watching eyes, and so forth.

Victims

The victims of white supremacy are those who are directly/indirectly impacted and disadvantaged by white supremacy. As mentioned earlier, all white people do not necessarily fit into the frame of white supremacy. Neither are all white people entitled to white privilege in its entirety. In fact, longstanding elite white supremacist look away in disgust at whites they deem as *poor white trash*; these individuals are at the bottom of the totem pole as impoverished blacks and other disadvantaged minorities. Many of these individuals reside in the south side of Baltimore City with the same issues of crime, drugs and poverty as the black inner-city Baltimoreans. The explanation of this is neither to inspire nor provoke sympathy; however, we should carefully examine which role we play in the system of white supremacy. Make no doubt about it, white supremacy is totally fixated on one's socioeconomic status and race. Usually those who fit the socioeconomic criteria and race demographics are entitled to the luxuries of white supremacy.

Children in the Inner-City of Baltimore

White supremacy can leave long lasting effects on our children's future. This impact can stem from the neighborhood and poverty, a schooling system, inadequate resources for advancement; all of these things are tools that white supremacist use to keep black people of the inner-city in a lower socioeconomic status or bracket. Generational welfare, poorly educated black families, poor health and healthcare facilities, repeat offenses leading to the incarceration of black men in the city, and a higher death rate than those who enjoy the benefits of white supremacist housing communities that ensure the best quality of living, the privilege of comfort, and police protection: these are all symptoms and signs of white supremacy working against its chosen opponents. It all boils down to equality. If our children are socioeconomically disadvantaged and purposely left

121

out of the margin of opportunity, they will repeat, reenact, and behave in the manner of those African Americans who are perpetual products of their poisonous environment. It is obvious that we must examine the condition of the inner-city of Baltimore and challenge our local government to do something about the present condition of the dilapidated housing structures, infamous drug trafficking, poor schooling, and insufficient resources.

As African Americans, we must also educate ourselves and challenge those who choose to participate in the system of white supremacy. Even those in the inner-city of Baltimore can partake in their own demise; and this too, fulfills the purpose of the white supremacist, who would much rather have blacks eradicate themselves through genocidal acts. We may not have control over the harassment we face when it comes to law enforcement; but we do have control over the way we govern ourselves and the types of activity we participate in. We must be mindful that incarceration of black people is the new form of slavery. Foster care is the new form of slavery for our black children. When we actively participate in types of behavior that enable us to be arrested or behavior that allow for the children's protective service to remove our children from our homes, we are killing ourselves and also keeping the institution of white supremacy strong with a vital Herculean pulse. We must beware of how we can become our own problem. White supremacy is a global terrorism. Blacks in America do get the worst end of white supremacy; however, we cannot rise above as a people, when we utilize the same behavior toward ourselves that the white supremacists use against us.

Denise Morris

CHAPTER 10

BLACK LIVES MATTER

Black Lives matter is a social activist organization and movement that focuses on the civil injustices, inequality, and mistreatment of black American's. These injustices range from a social, economic, political, racial, and white supremacist perspective. Black Lives Matter (BLM) emanated in 2013. Black Lives Matter was founded by Alicia Garza, Patrisse Cullors, and Opal Tometi. The death of black American teenager, Travon Martin, sparked the idea to create BLM to speak out against the social injustice that blacks in America face on a daily platform. Most recently they have went on to protest several other injustices against black Americans (i.e. Michael Brown, Eric Gardner, Tamir Rice, Philando Castro, and Alton Sterling to name a few) at the hands of law enforcement agents.

In 2015, BLM rallied and protested against the death of Baltimore's own, Freddie Gray; an African American male that was allegedly fatally injured while being arrested and detained by Baltimore City Police. This was also my first experience of living in a city where an ongoing riot was occurring. There was some much outrage and chaos taking place outside my home which is only a few blocks from Fulton Street, the actual origin or starting point of the 2015 Baltimore City riots. The National Guard and neighboring police task forces were call in patrol and protect particularly the affluent areas that generate money such as the downtown and Baltimore Inner Harbor areas. Many of these agencies set up shop in the Baltimore Ravens parking lot. Mayor Stephanie Rawlings-Blake had issued a curfew to control the protest and rioting. Mayor Rawlings-Blake also told the Baltimore Police Department to *stand down* and not pursue any further action against the rioting and protesting civilians after many police officers were injured in the midst of monitoring and policing the protestors. This order gave individuals who were not protesting an opportunity to loot, damage Baltimore's inner-city communities, and commit various other crimes. This scene was a combination of Armageddon, *The Purse*, Apocalypse, and a nostalgic moment in time that reminded us of the 60s riots. Furthermore, besides the areas of protest (Fulton Avenue and North Avenue) Baltimore City was totally devoid of police. You had to call the non-emergency line if you needed some type of assistance. It is very unusual not to hear a single police, ambulance, or fire truck siren screeching up and down the street. In fact, such noisy disturbances inform you that the city is awake. There were several helicopters in the sky; they were mainly used to track the movement of the rioters and protestors.

I witnessed the spark of the 2015 Baltimore riots at my job on monitor in my office. Apparently, the riots had just jumped off a few hours upon me leaving for work that following night. As I arrived home that next morning, I realized my front door handle to my apartment building had been broken off. I was totally unsure if someone were hiding in my building; therefore, I proceeded to enter with extreme apprehension and caution. Luckily, the vigorous barking of my puggle, Sol, reassured me that may home was devoid of intruders. I opened my apartment door as wide as possible and peeped from left to right before entering. My dog was anxiously waiting for me to enter. I entered my room first, and swung open the closet door, because that would be the only place an intruder could hide, since the rest of my room and apartment is mainly open space. A shear since of relief came over me as I thoroughly inspected my place. Helicopters were flying all over West Baltimore. I hesitated to take my dog outside to relieve herself. Being a dog, her senses were also amped. Sol refused to go outside toward the backyard to relieve herself. I did not bargain with her, and shut and secured my backdoor. My mobile phone was turned off the night before, because I do not receive reception at my work. When I finally turned on the phone, I realized there were over 20 missed calls, and about double that amount in text messages. They were mainly from family and loved ones back in my hometown, D.C. I had also received calls from relatives down south and friends up north. They had all spent the night watching the Baltimore riot on CNN, NBC, CBS, ABC, and any other major news broadcasting channel. News of the Baltimore riots really alarmed them. I first responded to those calls that were priority. My mother was glad to know that I was safe, and that I was nowhere in Baltimore on the night the riots had taken place. Then, I went down the line notifying my aunts, and other relatives of my whereabouts, and safety. With some much needed advice from my uncle that is now a retired D.C. policemen, I decided to stay home, and call off work. Judging by the ensuing angst and commotion going on outside my door, and the orders from the Mayor for the Baltimore police to stand down against responding to emergencies, I presumed we (Baltimoreans) were now in a state of martial law. Therefore, I retrieved my registered firearm, and sat on my bed with Sol, eagerly watching out for any intruders. That night, I was ready to kill at will or die. I was filled with anxiety, stress, and gloom. The thought of having to defend myself against the very people or persons who share my ethnicity, cultural customs, and societal struggles caused an uneasy and indescribable tension with inside me. However, that moment was really a state of Martial Law. I had to use the training and defense tactics I had acquired when I worked as an armed government agency contracting officer. Furthermore, I had to incorporate my scholarship and concentration in Criminal Justice Intelligence. The defense tactics, along with the academically acquired knowledge, came to use that night. Until that night, I have never fallen asleep with a firearm in my hand, and I hope I will never have be in a situation, where I may have to fatally injure a life in order to defend my own. Most importantly, I am ecstatic and overjoyed that no lives were lost that night, despite the looting and rioting, in the midst of what was mainly a peaceful protest.

Black Lives Matter Role in Baltimore

Following the death of Freddie Gray in April 2015, BLM organized statewide protests across the United States. The spirit of protest was far-reaching across all U.S. time zones. Despite, the media's attempt to sabotage the BLM's credibility, and declare the BLM protestors as thugs, disobedient, unlawful, and uncivil Americans, solidarity amongst various beings from various ethnic and cultural backgrounds, rallied in unison to convey the message that deliberate and systematic brutality at the hands of the law under the U.S. constitution is immoral, unjust, and unconstitutional. The Baltimore 2015 Riots lasted from the 18th of April 2015 until the 25th of April 2015.

I have never witnessed up close and personal, until this lifetime, so many youth actively partaking in a fight for civil liberty, and freedom. I have never had individuals both black and white, marching pass my window in harmony, and outrage against such a corrupt social system. Meanwhile, the media was busy posting catchy headlines about Baltimore "burning". As a Baltimore City inhabitant, I can honestly vouch that these burnings of property, though heinous, were exclusively limited to neighboring areas where the riots and protests ensured. The whole of Baltimore was not burning. The individuals that were looting and stealing, many did not live in the area, they were not

BLM activists and/or protestors, and they used the 2015 Baltimore riots as an opportunity to abuse the law. I, myself, did not engage in protest, however; BLM should not be held accountable for those individuals who violated the law while the riots were taking place. What really fueled the desire in those who had committed criminal activity, had nothing to do with BLM protest for Freddie Gray. It was actually the fact that they knew they would not be reprimanded (at least not during the riots) because Baltimore City police were given the mayor's order not to act or respond to that type of activity. It was clear and evident, judging by the news media coverage that these individuals looting shoes, liquor, toilet paper, household appliances, and other material, were not focused on BLM's civil demonstration. They acted in opposition of the movements objectives, and were not in the midst of the crowd of protestors. They were utilizing the police's visual and physical occupancy with crowd control to loot and damage nearby stores. Many natives, along with local media, stated that those individuals were not natives of Baltimore City. There are many conspiracy theories revolving around shadow powers paying individuals to stage an act to divert from whatever message a protesting organization or movement is trying to get across; especially, when that organization is capable of drawing attention to corruption that exposes government corruption.

Denise Morris

Black Lives Matter Focal Points

Those familiar with BLM, know that they have been the full
force of protest, against death and/or brutality of black
Americans at the hands of the law. They were originally founded
in 2013, and came together to protest against the death of
Trayvon Martin; a teenage black male, who was gunned down
by a white man, while walking from a local convenience store in
a majority white suburban community where his father resided.
The verdict of these case went in favor of the defendant who shot
Trayvon Martin, Andrew Zimmerman. Many in opposition of the
verdict, speculate that his acquittal is nothing more than white
supremacy at its best, considering the fact that his father is a
judge, and the actual judge in the case is in fact, a friend of
Zimmerman's father.

One the most recent fatal shootings of a black male, occurred
at the hands of Chicago police, on July 28, 2016. This is another
focal point of BLM activists. Many BLM supporters have been
hash tagging, commenting, and reposting via social media, the
actual police pursuit of 18 year-old Paul O'Neal, the young black
male who was gunned down by police in a manner that appears
to violate their police codes of conduct while pursuing a suspect.
The Chicago policemen can be seen irresponsibly discharging
their weapon in a residential neighborhood. The deliberate shots
fired at O'Neal (who fled the scene in a stolen car) were
unloaded in an unsafe, and incautious manner, without the least
regards for the residents or inhabitants of that housing

community. Bullets could have pierced through these residents' homes or in any direction where they were present, and injured them severely or mortally. These cops are going with the defense that O'Neal tried to hit the officers, while they stood barricaded by their squad cars. The bodycam of one of the officers reveal that the cop with that claim actually stepped in the presence of the fleeing vehicle. Furthermore, it is speculated by the attorney representing the now deceased O'Neal that one of the officers unlawfully shot O'Neal in the back, after capturing and beating him. Unfortunately, the bodycam for some mysterious reason, does not have any live footage of this. Many speculators believe that the police bodycam was intentionally turned off to protect the officers from being caught in the act of violating Mr. O'Neal's rights.

The backlash of BLMs focal point, arises through numerous news media attempts to discredit BLM's progress, by decrying the significance of the protested black individuals hat have been brutalized, and killed at the hands of law enforcement agents. White supremacist news media has succeeded in doing this through releasing the criminal records of these black individuals to try and justify the execution of these black individuals. Nearly all were unarmed, with the exception of the second most recent incident involving the fatal shooting of a 23 year-old black Baltimorean woman, Korryn Shandawn Gaines. This incident took place in Baltimore County on August 4, 2016. According to reports, and livestreaming of the event by Gaines herself, she was armed with a shotgun, and Baltimore City police endured hours of trying to negotiate with Gaines. Subsequently, this incident ended with Gaines being shot and killed by Baltimore County police. Gaines' 5 year-old son, was also reported shot by the cops as he attempted to free himself from the ordeal between the cops, and his mother. Ms. Gaines is reported to have been under mental distress, which may have allegedly been triggered from an argument that had ensued earlier that day between her and her boyfriend, who allegedly called the police on Gaines in attempts to diffuse the domestic dispute between the two.

Once again, the media eats these type of incidents up in order to exonerate the police from blame, reprimand, or prosecution. The news also takes to social media (e.g. Facebook, Twitter, Instagram, YouTube, etc.) to engage the general public to take sides with them on the matter. This is all an attempt to counter BLM's efforts to expose white supremacy, which imposes inequality, and fatal repercussions against black Americans via legislative, executive, and judicial system. Every day, individuals both black and white commit or participate in activity that may be deemed unlawful. However, blacks are pursued more aggressively, whether armed or not. Blacks are handled by the police in a questionable and unethical manner more frequently in comparison to white suspects. Black suspects in America have a higher percentage of being fatally injured by cops. It is neither a surprise nor myth that blacks are more susceptible to being targeted by cops, and handled by cops beyond the measures of the force continuum mandated by individual police districts.

BLM must devise and implement an effective socio-political strategy that goes beyond the range of protest. They must interpret the law and utilize the U.S. constitutional rights in their favor to rebut the media's attempts to negate the significant of the BLM movement. They must gather the vocal emphasis and social influence of their white supporters, to directly point out and challenge the system of white supremacy themselves; this way, actual white supremacist cannot deny the existence of white supremacy, because their own are in opposition and admitting to its existence alongside blacks who are being severely mishandled under the system of white supremacy. Marching and protesting is necessary, and should be used a social platform to promote the objectives of the organization in regards to how they plan to address these issues. These objectives should be framed in a manner that grabs the attention of the legislative, executive, and judicial bodies that work as one to ensure the value and prosperity of the U.S. constitutional amendments.

Black Lives Matter Vs. All Lives Matter

BLM has been opposed by individuals who feel as though the movement selfishly, and biasedly focuses on the significance of black lives. However, the imminence and reason for the movement is contrary to skeptics beliefs. BLM originated to draw emphasis to how black Americans are devalued, disenfranchised, easily violated, and excluded under the auspices of white supremacy. It is because of this exclusion and marginalization that BLM and participating activists black and non-black have joined as a whole from state to state, to elucidate the hypocrisy of a governmental body that claims to ensure rights for all of its citizens regardless of race. Even with the abolishment of traditional American slavery, the government has found a way to modernize its existence in order to keep blacks from advancing. The phrase '*All Lives Matter*' is shared and utilized by those who sympathize with a human struggle in general. These individuals seemingly believe that any injustice against any human being is an injustice. Another portion, utilize this phrase to downplay the existence of white supremacy, and its detriment toward people of color. Not be confused, because participants of white supremacy are black as well. Many of the black individuals that are doing this for the purpose of upholding white supremacy are doing it for political gain, social access/advancement, or they are simply being paid to carry out the agenda of white supremacist. The white supremacist utilization of the all lives matter phrase is to also shame BLM supporters, debunk, and dismantle. The way they achieve this is by declaring BLM activists as militant, anti-police, and anti-government. In essence, the idea is to perceive BLM as uncivil and disobedient revolutionaries that pose a threat to the U.S. constitution; therefore, they should be perceived ultimately as domestic terrorists, with the potential to motivate masses of followers from a global standpoint. So, the all lives matter phrase, from the white supremacist perspective is utilized to ultimately demobilize and de-globalize ideology or message of Black Lives Matter. This makes perfect sense, because if myriad races and cultures of individuals began to internalize and embrace Black Lives Matter ideology from a global perspective, white supremacy will be in danger of decreasing its power, and influence on a global scale. All Lives Matter phrase is a neutralizer that sides with those of genuine liberal stance; those that believe in the common good of all of humanity, and also those white supremacist that try, and pimp the phrase to try to counter target BLM as a black supremacist movement. The latter is highly unlikely, considering the supremacy means having extreme and total control, until the point where the lesser is totally dominated by those with supreme authority, and abjectly subordinate to that supreme groups order. Therefore, black supremacy cannot co-exist with white supremacy, because only one or the other can be in total power at once. We (citizens of America) are all under a white supremacist social infrastructure. Luckily, the various ethnicities a part of and in support of the BLM, helps disprove the notion that they are a black supremacist domestic terrorist organization.

Denise Morris

Black Lives Matter Influence Amongst the People

BLM has managed to capture the attention of people from various walks of life. As mentioned earlier, they have the support and backing of white individuals who recognize that there is a definite imbalance in justice and equally, when it comes to blacks in America. They also have Latino/a, Asian, Indian, and other minority individuals rallying in support of the movement. All of these races represent the mosaic culture of America and all of its ethnic diversity. Entertainers have even shown there support of BLM's objective to stand tall against the brutalization of the black community. Black rappers, black athletes, black movie stars, and black humanitarians have motivated their fans of all creeds to participate in the struggle for civil equality for blacks in America. The voices of these entertainers electrically charged the passion and courage within their colleagues that were at first reluctant join countless others in a divine effort to inspire and/or provoke change. For too long, celebrities, particularly and especially black celebrities, have been afraid to exercise their voice toward a cause that would also benefit them, and their loved ones. Many feared of losing endorsements, wealth, their careers, sponsors, and fan base. Their fears are reasonable and understandable. No one wants to risk their livelihood and some they've worked so hard to gain.

I remember watching a HBO documentary/interview of one of the greatest black boxers, Floyd Mayweather. He had to do jail time after to one of his fights. Everyone either hates or loves his cocky personality. He is known for traveling with hundreds of thousands in cash. He throws the money up in strip clubs, takes his friends and family on luxurious trips, and shopping. He is what white America refers to as young, black, and flashy. Many boxing commentators have challenged his cocky bravado during fights. Nonetheless, he remains undefeated throughout his whole boxing career. Heavy is the head that bears the crown. Greater is the challenge for the one who righteously accepts their plight. During the interview, the journalist asked Floyd of his greatest challenge while being incarcerated. Floyd replied that not being able to be free and do as he pleased. He went on to say that he had millions in the bank, but he could do nothing with it, because he was in prison. He learned the great value of what matters most over money and wealth; freedom. Freedom is the ultimate God given wealth, and power.

The entertainers of color that took a stand with BLM realized the same thing as Floyd Mayweather. They realized that it is worth more to compromise money and fame, than to compromise your integrity, race, and freedom. It is no coincidence that many of these entertainers are controlled and closely monitored by predominantly white male patriarchal supremacist industries, franchises, and corporations. This is the main reason why so many have not step forth in support of BLM or any movement that may exonerate them from social and racial inequality. Although many of these black wealthy celebrities have faced the same injustices and gotten a wake-up call, some are so content on maintaining their wealth. Floyd Mayweather's wake-up call that came to him as he sat in prison as a wealthy, yet, an incarcerated man in the cells of a white supremacist prison system, should be a lesson to these black stars, that until you speak out against the system of oppression, you will only remain a rich slave. Money does not grant blacks in America sovereignty. Under white supremacy, blacks will always be vilified, victimized, ostracized, and may even be killed. Social media shows like *TMZ* stalk black celebrities, with hopes to catch them in a frenzy of illegal activity, and deviant mischief. It should be no surprise that the CEO, Harvey Levin, is a Jewish lawyer. Levin's trash journalists operate like spies for the law enforcement agency. Then they make fun of these celebrities' legal situations and personal issues, as if, they are soulless fiends. Needless to say, there are many black entertainers who live for this type of hype and exploitation. These types of individuals can care less that we are in the midst of another black civil rights era.

Carmelo Anthony

Carmelo Anthony, New York Knicks power forward, and Baltimore native, took a stance and challenged his fellow teammates, and colleagues to do so as well. During the 2016 ESPY awards, Carmelo spoke out concerning the police multiple shootings of blacks, and even the killing of cops. He also marched to Baltimore's City Hall during the time of the

Baltimore riots in April 2015. Meanwhile, there are very wealthy and famous other black stars that are natives of Baltimore that did not partake in protest, during the Baltimore 2015 riots. We've witnessed one of these stars go on a social media rant, because her husband did not receive an Oscar for his "dynamic role" in his movie entitled *Concussion*. Her tireless rant, alone, was enough to give the whole entire city of Baltimore a concussion. Needless to say, she did not show up to march for the injustice and murder of Freddie Gray. Carmelo demonstrated his solidarity for his hometown. He represented the youth of Baltimore that stood up to injustice, and marched to grab the attention of Baltimore officials, to right the wrongs of a corrupt local government that turns deaf ears and blind eyes when it comes to police brutality of Baltimore's blacks (those specifically within the inner-city).

Ray Lewis

Retired Baltimore Ravens defensive player, Ray Lewis, sent what white media declared a "powerful" and "emotional" message, from his Florida home via social media. Many Baltimoreans would agree, he could have shown more respect for his Baltimore fans that have shown him love, and worshipped him as if he were pharaoh or Zeus. His message appeared more as a black athlete, acting as a white supremacist sycophant agent in attempts to diverge Baltimore youth, from standing tall against a crooked law enforcement system. The youth of Baltimore do

139

not need a black pacifist dissuading them from making a political statement for the world to see. Lewis came off as an angry house servant that felt the need to bring order to the field slaves (Baltimore protesting youth), in order to appease Master (corrupt Baltimore government, and law enforcement housed under white supremacy). Lewis, of all people, should know and understand that a change cannot ensue, without the ruffling of the feathers of the very system that brought about the trouble in the first place. Just as Lewis magnificently utilized his defensive tactics, to bustle his way through the offensive line of the opposing team to make a tackle or sack, so shall the same strategy be exercised by our youth upon a political platform. His aggravated tone did not stop the agenda at hand. We cannot tell our children to hush and sit down, when their freedoms are capable of being violated on a daily basis, by the very individuals put in place to protect those freedoms.

George Soros

This name may ring as unfamiliar to the countless participants and protestors within the Black Lives Matter movement. However, this name is the key token to the maneuverability of the leaders and organizers of the movement. George Soros, originally born as Gyorgy Schwartz, is a Jewish Hungarian that was born in the most crucial times of the Nazi movement and the Great Depression era. According to various sources, Soros parents fled Hungary to avoid being captured, detained, and even killed by the Nazi militia under the reign of Hitler. To make a long story short, Mr. Soros was brought to America and engaged in banking occupations, and became a successful financial investor of Wall Street. Mr. Soros is also a self-proclaimed millionaire, and the financial muscle behind the Black Lives Matter movement. Critics may ask, what would a non-black person of Jewish descent want with supporting and advocating the rights of a group of individuals, who have faced a lifetime of social inequality in American since their inception and introduction in the Americas. Conspiracy theorists, project that Soros is supporting the movement only to globalize the hatred of blacks through social media, and make them a target for white supremacist groups. Realist suggest that Soros is truly acting out of kindness and an incarnation to fight for the cause of blacks because he empathizes with the social plight of blacks due to the atrocities his people suffered in the Holocaust era at the hands of the notorious dictator, Hitler. Many black consciousness advocates, purpose the notion that no genuine good deed could come out of a Jewish or white person backing a black civil movement. Most of the speculation is deep rooted in the negative stigma that Jewish individuals are deceptive, self-promoting, money-hungry, and untrustworthy. Hitler's hatred toward the Jews (although Hitler's mother was Jewish) personified such a distasteful stereotype in the hearts and minds of many individuals who share a strong dislike toward Jewish persons. Regardless of the resentment of the Black Lives Matter

141

movement or the advocacy thereof, the true intentions of the Black Lives Matter movement maybe solely contingent upon the overall outcome, the results or success. Black Lives Matter can be more structured and organized; considering the fact that the movement is supported by such a financially astute source.

Could it be that the conspiracy theorists are correct. Black Lives Matter activist, DeRay McKesson, has been accused of starting go-fund-me accounts under the auspices of funding the Black Lives Matter movement. However, individuals exclaim it is merely a scheme for Mr. McKesson to line his pockets with Black Lives Matter sympathizer's hard-earned dollars. To add more fuel to the fire, Mr. McKesson made a last minute attempt to run in the April 26, 2016 Baltimore democratic primaries for Baltimore City mayor. Critics will declare the his immediate involvement in the Black Lives Matter movement, and his arbitrary attempt to run for Baltimore mayor is all a part of his scheme for a political upgrade, and financial comeuppance. On the contrary, those who are a tad more familiar with McKesson's background, will declare him a scholar, youth advocate, educator, and a Baltimorean who understands the needs of Baltimore City. His bio reveals that his activism started way before the existence of the Black Lives Matter movement. He is also a part of the future and present leaders of Baltimore City. It would be devastating if his dealings were insincere. He has been criticized because of his sexual orientation, political affiliation, and actual political motives. Although he has somewhat of an elaborate activism resume, his premise on black lives is yet to be verbally addressed. Protesting is the way to gain attention and platform in order to introduce outlined objectives as a solution. However, what is the premise. Is it protesting against the brutalization of blacks at the hands of police or law enforcement agents? Is it a more in depth issue entailing the social and economic inequality when it comes to blacks and whites? Is it the overall systematic depravation of blacks under the microscope of white supremacy? All the above? Protest without premise obscures the actual motives and reasons for the existence of Black Lives Matter founders. Protest is meant to be heard and seen in order to move to the next level of getting actual results. Skeptics within the black community do not believe that it is possible to achieve this when this Black Lives Matter organization is monetarily funded by a Jewish philanthropist. Many feel that the movement is funded to gather a flock of agitators to deflect from the progress of achieving justice for blacks in America when it comes to law enforcement brutality.

Regardless of Black Lives Matter movement issues, black lives do matter. Anyone champion the matters of black lives respectively and constructively give breath to the concerns that effect all black lives no matter the economic situation. Both wealthy and poor blacks are subjected to the same racial treatment in America. In America, skin color trumps one's financial stance. White skin equals white privilege and

143

Denise Morris

protection under the constitution. This should come as no surprise since the U.S. Constitution was written by white patriarchal male supremacist slaveholders and enslavers.

Chapter 11

MOVING FORWARD

By the time this book is published, a new mayor will be in office in Baltimore city. Most of the conditions (dilapidated communities, failing city school system, drugs, and poverty) in the inner will probably go unimproved. One would think, a mayor selected by the people, who is a member of the black race, would identify with the social ills of the community from experience, and strive to do more. This remains to be seen. It is possible that the new mayor elect will be the contrast of what Baltimore does not need, and the champion of the inner-city community. However, when this person is already ridiculed before entering the office, hopes of a better Baltimore city dulls. It is rather poor political strategy, and a degrading pursuit to lure poor black people of color into voting, by buying them fried chicken, and putting them on a party bus to attend the voting poles. You cannot start a term with deception. Especially, when the requirements for the position under which you serve requires you to be transparent, honest, ethical, and a leader. Politics throughout America has never been so clean-cut, and Baltimore has never been known for its genteel treatment of its black population.

Denise Morris

Aside from the upcoming mayor, the city of Baltimore has to deal with a changing police force. Myself, along with many other black members of Baltimore's inner-city have noticed the changes faces in law enforcement. The "boys in blue" are looking less and less like the members of the community. I have encountered quite a few who express disdain and contempt toward the individuals they are meant to protect and serve. Baltimore city has a lot of younger white adult male and females. A great majority of these individuals do not live in Baltimore, and are very unfamiliar with dealings with people of color. Considering their background and cultural upbringing, many of these young white police officers have not experienced daily social interactions with black people until they decided to become a part of Baltimore city's police department. This is not a good look for several reasons. Reason oné, individuals unfamiliar with black culture (especially unfamiliar whites) are likely to harshly scrutinize and misjudge blacks, and police communities, according to negative stereotypes that criminalize all black individuals regardless of their individual status. Reason two, there is more likely a change for increased racial profiling due to some white cops stereotyping and prejudging black individuals of Baltimore's inner-city. For instance, an older friend of mines, nearly 60 years of age, was profiled on his way to a local carryout in my neighborhood. What is normally a 15 minute trip turned into nearly an hour commute, because he was stopped, and frisked by two young white male police officers, who have no idea who is a noble member of the community, and who is an actual threat. They made him empty his pockets, and asked him where he was going, and did not inform him of why he had been stopped. When he asked the officers why, they exclaimed the typical you "fit the profile" of a black male suspect we got a call about. Really. This alleged suspect supposedly committed some unlawful act and fled on foot. They did not say whether the black unknown suspect was described as old or young. Nor did they tell my friend that he had on any similar clothing to the suspect. All of which makes one assume that their reason for stopping him was bogus, and nonetheless, racial profiling. They did not use their better judgement to realize that this man is old enough to be their elder. They cornered him, made him empty his pockets, and sit on the filthy Baltimore city ground. This incident leads to another initial reason why cops who do not identify or relate to the people of the black community should not be qualified to police the black community. As a counseling psychology graduate scholar, myself, and other counseling psychology graduates have to take a mandatory course on multiculturalism and cultural sensitivity. The reason being, is because we have to be cognizant of clients from all walks of life's cultural profile, and be able to identify the counseling needs of individuals who come from unique, and diversified backgrounds. The same was required of me when I was studying criminal justice intelligence in my bachelors

Denise Morris

program. As a criminal intelligence potential professional or
student you are required to understand the criminal natures, and
dealings with other races or minorities in order to determine the
difference between a threat, versus apprehensive speculation,
based around negatives stereotypes of certain subgroups and
ethnic groups. Numerous times, I have encountered those
specific white Baltimore cops who have followed me home, and
decided to stop and harass me for no apparent reason. There was
a time when I did government security, and I had on my entire
uniform with my government credentials attached to my uniform
BDUs, and those officers still had the nerve to ask me what am I
doing, when I was simply arriving home from work, and parking
my car to go in the house. Their holding me up had no specific
rhyme or reason. Just like my friend's encounter, these white
cops did not inform me of a legitimate reason as to why I was
being stopped. One of the officers made up a lie about my tail
light, and wrote me a work order for repair. To my surprise, all
of my lights worked fine when I took my vehicle to the mechanic
for service. In spite of this, I still had to have the mechanic sign
off and confirm my lights where working properly. I also had to
waste my gas, and drive out of the city to the Maryland State
Police to turn in the order, and have my lights inspected by a
Maryland State Trooper. The spite of the white cops that are
racist is uncanny. They will subject you to nonsense even if they
do not have anything on you. There are more seasoned white
Baltimore city officers who understand the community, and do

not treat the blacks in the community this way. Most of them know the inhabitants of their assigned community by name, and they are even familiar with the common neighborhood criminals. Unfortunately, many of these officers have served their time, and countless others have retired. The Baltimore city police department is now being phased out with uninformed, culturally biased, and bigoted young white officers. While I do not exclaim this is the case for all of the newer white Baltimore officers; myself, and other blacks can attest that the dealings with these types of cops are becoming more and more frequent. The Freddie Gray incident, and the Baltimore Riots of 2015 were a direct response to the maltreatment of blacks by law enforcement. Mayor Stephanie Rawlings-Blake was criticized horribly by the black community for how she handle the riots. The district attorney, Marilyn Mosby, was also verbally torn to shreds by the black community, and reprimanded with a lawsuit by the officers she tried to prosecute in the Freddie Gray case. Her professional environment, filed a lawsuit against her to shame her, and scorn her for stepping out of compliance with a unspoken code of honor that places law enforcement, and the judicial system before the needs of the people; particularly black people. In my belief, I am not sure if there was much Mrs. Mosby could have done to bring those six officers to justice. As we turn on the news, we see countless blacks being slaughtered at the hands of the police nationwide. Their deaths are being recorded, and made viewable on YouTube and other social media networks. Many black leaders, and black historians refer to these shootings as modern day lynchings. To witness the constant brutal and fatal treatment of blacks via law enforcement is psychologically damaging, emotionally, and spiritually traumatizing. It also sends a foul message to America that black lives are not of importance in a white supremacist society, where we blacks are constantly targeted, and many annihilated.

One must ask whether or not the upcoming mayor would address these issues in Baltimore's inner-city. Will she ignore the degradation of the black condition due to racial inequality? Would she practice *benign neglect* and tiptoe around failing social, and economic conditions of the black Baltimore inner-city? Many politicians' strong speaking points are based upon their past political contributions. Many believe Pugh will not hold up as mayor and sit back to relish in a position that she acquired based upon the "old things" the people know of her. Baltimore cannot afford to have an elusive council member with the ability to change the conditions of the city, sit back and turn deaf ears upon those who have elected her to mobilize our dilapidated communities. Nonetheless, many Baltimoreans are hopeful toward a brighter outcome. They are hopeful to have a mayor that would be vocal and demonstrative as far as her intentions for improving Baltimore are concerned. The black community needs a mayor that is going to be integral and encouraging to those blacks who are trying to pave their way in a city that is beautiful, unique, and damaged by political ignorance, and corruption in the same breath.

Denise Morris

References

Barber, C. N. (2003). Parent-adolescent relationship and
  adolescent psychological functioning
   among African-American female adolescents: self-
  esteem as a mediator. *Journal Of Child And Family
  Studies*, (3), 361.
Barrett, P. M., Webster, H. M., & Wallis, J. R. (1999).
  Adolescent self-esteem and cognitive
  skills training: a school-based intervention. *Journal Of
  Child And Family Studies,* (2), 217.
Depression. (2016). Retrieved February 2, 2016, from
  https://www.nami.org/Learn-
  more/Mental-Health-Conditions/Depression.
Hacker. 2016. *Merriam-Webster.com*. Retrieved February
  1, 2016, from http://www.merriam-
  Webster.com/dictionary/hacker.
Harden, K., Tucker-Drob, E., & Tackett, J. (n.d). The
  Texas Twin Project. *Twin Research And
  Human Genetics*, 16(1), 385-390.
Hartinger-Saunders, R. M., Rine, C. M., Nochajski, T., &
Wieczorek, W. (2012). Neighborhood
  crime and perception of safety as predictors of
  victimization and offending among youth:
  A call for macro-level prevention and intervention
  models. *Children And Youth Services Review*, 341966-
  1973. doi:10.1016/j.childyouth.2012.05.020
Hirsch, B. J., Mickus, M., & Borger, R. (2002). Ties to
  influential adults among Black and White
  adolescents: Culture, social class, and family
  networks (1). *American Journal Of
  Community Psychology*, (2), 289.
LeCroy, C. W., & Daley, J. (2001). Empowering
  building skills for the future with the Go Grrrls Program.
  New York: W. W. Norton.
Mann, H., Garcia-Rada, X., Houser, D., & Ariely, D.
  (2014). Everybody Else Is Doing It:
  Exploring Social Transmission of Lying Behavior. *Plos
  ONE*, 9(10), 1. doi:10.1371/journal.pone.0109591.
Michalak, J., Tobias, T., Thomas, H., Gunnar, T., & Vocks,

S. (2011). Buffering low self-esteem: and depression. *Personality And Individual Differences*. (50), 751-754.

Okwumabua, J., Wong, S., Duryea, E., Okwumabua, T., & Howell, S. (1999). Building Self-Esteem Through Social Skills Training and Cultural Awareness: A Community-Based Approach for Preventing Violence Among African American Youth. *Journal Of Primary Prevention, 20(1)*, 61. doi:10.1023/A:1021306502993.

Okeke-Adeyanju, N., Taylor, L. C., Craig, A. B., Smith, R. E., Thomas, A., Boyle, A. E., & DeRosier, M. E. (2014). Celebrating the strengths of black youth: increasing self-esteem and implications for prevention. *The Journal Of Primary Prevention*, 35(5), 357-369. doi:10.1007/s10935-014-0356-1.

Peterson, S. H. (2007). The Importance of Fathers: Contextualizing Sexual Risk-Taking in "Low-risk" African American Adolescent Girls. *Journal Of Human Behavior In The Social Environment*, 15(2/3), 329-346. doi:10.1300/J137v15n02_19.

Prince, D. L., & Howard, E. M. (2002). Children and Their Basic Needs. Early Childhood Education Journal, 30(1), 27-31.

Prelow, H. M., Weaver, S. R., & Swenson, R. R. (2006). Efficacy as Mediators of Ecological Risk and Depressive Symptoms in Urban African American and European American Youth. *Journal Of Youth And Adolescence*, 35(4), 506-516.

Rosenberg, M. (1965). Society and the adolescent self-University Press.

Rosenberg, M. (1979). Conceiving the Self. Basic Books,

Rosenberg, M., Schooler, C., Schoenbach, C., and Rosenberg, F. (1995). Global self esteem and specific self-esteem: Different concepts, different outcomes. Am. *Social Rev*. 60:141-156.

Saunders, J., Davis, L., Williams, T., & Williams, J. H. (2004). Gender Differences in Self-Perceptions and Academic Outcomes: A Study of Students. *Journal Of Youth And Adolescence*, 33(1), 81.

153

Denise Morris

Seaton, E. K. (2010). The Influence of Cognitive
    Discrimination on the Psychological Well-Being of
    African American Youth. *Journal Of Youth And
    Adolescence*, 39(6), 694-703.
Seaton, E. K., & Yip, T. (2009). School and neighborhood
    American adolescents. Journal of Youth and
    Adolescence, 38, 153–163.
Street, J., Harris-Britt, A., & Walker-Barnes, C. (2009).
Examining Relationships Between
    Ethnic Identity, Family Environment, and Psychological
Outcomes for African American
    Adolescents. *Journal Of Child & Family Studies*, 18(4),
    412.doi:10.1007/s10826-008-9245-7.
van Laar, C. (2000). The Paradox of Low Academic
    Achievement but High Self-Esteem in
    African American Students: An Attributional Account.
    Educational Psychology Review, (1). 33.